THE POCKET GUIDE TO
BIRDS OF EASTERN
NORTH AMERICA

THE POCKET GUIDE TO
BIRDS OF EASTERN NORTH AMERICA

Frank Shaw

DRAGON'S WORLD

Dragon's World Ltd
Limpsfield
Surrey RH8 0DY
Great Britain

First published by Dragon's World 1990

Illustrations by Norman Arlott, Trevor Boyer, Malcolm Ellis,
Robert Morton, Maurice Pledger, Christopher Rose and David Thelwell of
Bernard Thornton Artists, London.

British Library Cataloguing in Publication Data

Shaw, Frank
  The pocket guide to birds of eastern north America.
  1. North America. Eastern North America. Birds
  I. Title
  598.297

ISBN 1-85028-092-4

Editor: Michael Downey
Designer: Peter Ward
Editorial Director: Pippa Rubinstein

Typeset by Action Typesetting Ltd, Gloucester, England
Printed in Singapore

Contents

Introduction

The field guide had its origins in America in the 1930s and, for twenty or so years, remained exclusively a North American concept. Only in the 1950s did the idea migrate across the Atlantic to Europe. Today, field guides cover not only many different parts of the world, but many different subjects. There are, for example, guides to flowers, insects, mammals, amphibians and reptiles, fungi, as well as – among other subjects – pond life, archeology and buildings. Yet the whole thing started with Roger Tory Peterson's passion for birds, and birds remain the single most important subject of field guides.

The appeal of the bird field guide is readily understood. The aim is simple, to enable anyone to put a name to any bird they may see in a defined area. To this end, the contemporary field guide illustrates every species in color and a complementary text highlights the points by which each bird can be identified.

As bird identification has become more sophisticated, the size of field guides has, quite naturally, tended to grow in size. So, authors, artists and designers have sought ways in which an increasing number of different birds can be fitted on to a page. The result is often a guide that is either light on text, light on illustrations, or both. In this guide, however, we have intentionally given every bird a full half page, making full use of the space available for both text and illustration. Yet, at the same time, the book has remained small enough to be pocketable.

In order to make the most of the book's size, we have restricted this volume's scope to those birds that can be expected in the eastern half of North America. A companion volume covers the birds that can be expected in the west. Each volume is self-sufficient and, for that reason, there is a degree of overlap. Nevertheless, anyone interested in the birds of the whole of North America should have both the east and the west guides, although it will usually only be necessary to carry one with you in the field. This not only makes the individual guide more portable but, being geographically restricted, makes an individual bird easier to find.

We have also restricted each guide to the birds that the regular birder can expect to encounter. Thus we have omitted European waifs that have, on occasion, managed to struggle across the Atlantic, as well as western birds that have occasionally managed to wander eastwards into our area. We have also eliminated several southern species that may be found along the Rio Grande, in south-western Texas, but which are never seen elsewhere in North America. Together, these factors have reduced the scope of the two guides combined to about 630 distinct species. Or, put another way, we have omitted about 200 of the birds that have, on occasion managed to be seen, but which cannot in any sense be regarded as North American. In practice, every bird that any birder is likely to see is included.

In drawing the boundary between east and west, we have used the foothills of the Rocky Mountain system as the most obvious feature. In general, typically eastern birds extend no further, while typically western birds stop short of the great plains. The boundary starts in the south, roughly half way along the Texas-Mexico border, cuts through the panhandle of Oklahoma, through eastern Colorado, Wyoming and Montana before entering Canada at the Saskatchewan-Alberta border. It slices across the southern and western part of the latter before running roughly parallel with, and just east, of the Yukon border, reaching the Beaufort Sea at Mackenzie. No less than 435 distinct species of birds are of regular occurrence east of this line. These are the subjects of this guide.

The birds are arranged in the scientific, or systematic, order adopted by all serious books and publications. Beginners often have difficulty in finding their way around this arrangement and argue that it would be better to arrange birds alphabetically, or according to size, or even habitat. While there is some force to this argument, it is relatively easy to learn the basic structure of the systematic order by using it frequently. After a while it becomes second nature to look for herons near the front, gulls in the middle and sparrows at the end. This systematic approach has, however, one overwhelming advantage − by grouping similar species together, it shows the relationships between birds. Thus, if one sees a heron it is a simple matter to flick through the pages and find all the herons placed together.

Each bird has a scientific, as well as an English, name. The names used here follow the American Ornithologists' Union Check List of 1983, though more recent changes have been incorporated and we have followed the general movement towards a standardized list of English names for all the birds in the world. Thus we use the name American Robin rather than plain Robin; Common Redpoll rather than Redpoll. Eventually, there will be a universally accepted list of English names. We hope that, in the meantime, the use of these 'qualifying' adjectives will become more widely used.

Identifying birds is partly an art and partly a science, the key is knowledge. Confronted by an unknown bird, the secret of identification is knowing what to look for. This knowledge can be acquired from books, or by actively pursuing birds in the field. As with so many other skills, a combination of the two is probably the best method. Learning that gulls are often identified by their wing tips; that shorebirds require close attention to be paid to their rump patterns; that flycatchers can be divided by the presence or absence of wing-bars and eye-rings and so on, can be learned without ever setting sight on a bird. But there is no substitute for practice with the actual bird before one's binoculars.

Some birds are easily identified and quickly become familiar. Others, often because they are seen less frequently, remain a problem. Carrying around a field guide at all times is a vital element in the learning process. It enables every bird seen to be correctly named, but it also acts as a source of background knowledge when checking an unknown locality, or exploring a new habitat. Always remember that not all birds are as widely distributed as the Robin, nor are they so catholic in their choice of habitat as the Starling. Spotting a Kirtland's Warbler in a Texas backyard is about as likely as seeing an Acorn Woodpecker in Central Park, New York. Birds are creatures of habit and knowing as much as possible about their habits can prevent mistakes.

The field guide also acts as a crammer, a means by which one can learn in advance what to look for in particular birds. Using a field guide as bed-time reading every night is a sure method of getting to know unfamiliar birds, though it may not be conducive to sleep. Puzzling through the warblers and flycatchers can exercise the best of minds, but there is no better method of learning their field marks. Similarly, bus, train and plane journeys all offer opportunities to 'mug-up' particular bird groups.

Just where bird identification moves from the field of science (knowledge) to art (feeling) is difficult to say. Perhaps it varies from person to person. Somewhere along the line, however, it becomes instinct and it is possible to name birds at a glance, often without seeing a single field mark. Such skill is the result of a combination of knowledge and experience. Suddenly an accipiter becomes an accipiter, rather than a confusing bird of prey on the pages of the field guide. A crane is a crane, not a heron; a warbler a warbler not a sparrow; a jaeger a jaeger, not an immature gull. Somehow, a sense of a bird's character has been acquired − a combination of shape, structure and behavior that is unique to a particular bird enables it to be identified instantly and at great distance. This is birding as an art and, therefore, difficult to define or explain. To the beginner it seems impossible to acquire such skill, but never despair − the rule is learn and practice.

Top birders are obsessed. But even if you have no ambitions to be a top birder and just do not seem able to catch the obsession, don't worry. Birding is a lovely way of spending time. Not everyone can be a Gary Player or a Jack Nicklaus, but that does not stop millions of Americans beating a ball around a golf course every weekend. Enjoy your birding.

All birds depicted are adult males in summer plumage with the exception of the three phalaropes, which are female.

Common Loon Great Northern Diver

Gavia immer 27–37in/68–81cm

Identification A large, duck-like bird that dives easily. In summer, black head and boldly checkered back separate from all divers except Yellow-billed Loon which has pale ivory bill. In winter, back is barred gray and large, pointed, black bill is held horizontally. White extends above eye. *See* Yellow-billed Loon.
Voice Wild wailing cries in summer.
Habitat Lakes in summer; coasts in winter.
Range Breeds throughout Canada to US borders.
Movements Winters west and east coasts of Canada and US, including Gulf Coast.

Arctic Loon

Gavia arctica 23–27in/58–68cm

Black throated Diver

Identification In summer, distinguished by gray crown, black throat, checkered back and boldly striped neck. In winter is the darkest of all the loons, with dark crown extending to below the eye. At this time most likely to be confused with the Common Loon, but white patch on rear flank can be helpful.
Voice Loud wailings in summer.
Habitat Large lakes in summer; coasts in winter.
Range Breeds throughout Alaska, eastwards through Canadian arctic, south of tree line.
Movements Winters west coast of Canada and US.

Red-throated Loon

Gavia stellata 21–23in/53–58cm

Red-throated Diver

Identification Smallest of the loons. In summer, has gray head with rusty throat and striped nape and hind neck. At this season, is only loon that lacks checker-board back. In winter is grayer above than other loons. Thin bill always held uptilted.
Voice Wailing and cackling in summer.
Habitat Breeds on small lakes moving to sea or larger lakes to feed; winters along coasts.
Range Breeds coastal and tundra Canada.
Movements Moves southwards to winter on east and west coasts and along southern shores of Great Lakes.

Western Grebe

Aechmophorus occidentalis 22–29in/56–74cm

Identification Largest of grebes, with exceptionally long neck and bill. Upper parts dark gray, extending up hind neck to form a black cap that is curiously 'bumped' at rear. White 'face' and foreneck prominent at a distance. In flight, shows white bar across wing. Elaborate dancing display.

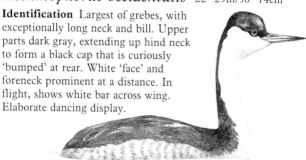

Voice *Kr-r-rick,* especially in summer.
Habitat Lakes in summer; coasts in winter.
Range Breeds on lakes of the west as far as the prairie lakes.
Movements Winters along west coast of British Columbia and the US as far as Mexico.

Red-necked Grebe
Podiceps grisegena
15½–18in/40–46cm

Identification Medium-
sized grebe. In summer,
black cap, silvery 'face'
and rust-red neck
are distinctive. In
winter, a black cap,
whitish 'face' and dusky foreneck are best identification features.
Size and substantial bill should separate from smaller grebes at all
times.
Voice Wailing and loud *keck-keck* when breeding.
Habitat Lakes with plentiful emergent vegetation; mainly coastal
in winter.
Range Breeds from Alaska to the Great Lakes in Canada and to
the US border country.
Movements Some birds migrate across the eastern US to winter
along the Atlantic coasts; others winter along Pacific coasts as far
south as California.

Horned Grebe
Podiceps auritus 12–14in/31–36cm

Identification A colorful grebe in
summer with black head and golden
'horns' extending as a crest. Foreneck
and underparts are rust-red. In winter,
dark above and white below with
distinctive capped appearance and
white foreneck. Bill thickish and
pointed. *See* Eared Grebe.
Voice Various squealing notes.
Habitat Marshy lakes and ponds
in summer; coastal in winter.
Range Breeds over most of western Canada, except extreme north.
Movements Migrates across northern US to winter on Atlantic
coasts, along Central Flyway to Gulf Coast and along Pacific coast
as far as California.

Eared Grebe
Podiceps nigricollis
11–13in/28–33cm

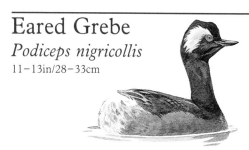

Identification Only a trifle smaller than Horned Grebe. In summer, head and neck black, with a gold fan on sides of 'face'. Breast black, underparts and flanks rusty. In winter, is dark above and white below. Cap darkish with paler hind crown, foreneck dusky not white as Horned Grebe. Bill, thin and uptilted at all times.
Voice Quiet *poo-cep* plus various raucous notes.
Habitat Marshes and ponds in summer; winters on coasts and large lakes.
Range Breeds in prairie zone of western Canada southwards over much of western US.
Movements Winters along Pacific coast, but many move southwards into Mexico.

Pied-billed Grebe
Podilymbus podiceps
12–15in/30–38cm

Identification A thick-set, chunky grebe with large conical bill. Upperparts brown, with boldly barred brown and buff flanks and square-cut white rear end. In summer, there is a bold black patch on the throat and the heavy, pale bill has a vertical black bar near the tip. In winter, throat and bill are both whitish. Pale eye-ring at all times.
Voice Various yelping calls.
Habitat Shallow ponds with vegetation in summer; plus larger waters in winter.
Range Breeds throughout US and southern Canada.
Movements Leaves northern and central parts of range in winter.

Least Grebe
Tachybaptus dominicus 8–10in/20–25cm

Identification Tiny grebe with
dusky gray head, neck and
upperparts in summer, but barred
buffy on flanks. Bold yellow eye
and tiny dark bill are best field
marks. In winter, upperparts are
less dusky and throat is white.
Voice Distinctive clanging note.
Habitat Overgrown ponds.
Range Breeds southern Texas;
but distinctly local.
Movements Resident.

Northern Fulmar
Fulmaris glacialis
17–19½in/44–50cm

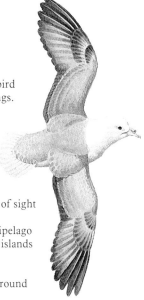

Identification A large, gull-like seabird
that flies, shearwater-like, on stiff wings.
Pale gray above, white below with
a short, stubby yellow bill. At
all times the thick neck is a
good feature.
Voice Harsh cackling at
breeding sites.
Habitat Breeds on remote northern
cliffs, otherwise at sea, often well out of sight
of land.
Range Breeds among Canadian archipelago
as far south as Newfoundland and on islands
of southern Alaska.
Movements Winters in Pacific and
northern Atlantic, may be abundant around
fishing vessels.

Audubon's Shearwater F
Puffinus plherminieri
11–12in/28–30cm

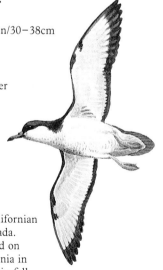

Identification Small shearwater
that is black above and white below;
has black undertail coverts, but these
are virtually impossible to see in the
field. Shorter, more rounded wings
than other shearwaters, with fluttering
more murre-like flight. Only confusable
with rarer Manx Shearwater, but bill
tiny in comparison.
Voice Silent at sea.
Habitat Oceans.
Range Regular visitor to Florida and east coast of US.
Movements Disperses from breeding grounds in Bahamas.

Manx Shearwater
Puffinus puffinus 12–15in/30–38cm

Identification A typical shearwater
that careers over the sea showing
alternately black upperparts
and white underparts.
Could be confused with
Audubon's Shearwater, but
is larger, longer-winged and less
fluttering in flight.
Voice Silent at sea.
Habitat Oceans.
Range Regular offshore along Californian
coast, rare off coast of eastern Canada.
Movements Breeds in Europe and on
islands off the coast of Baja California in
Mexico. Mostly in North America in fall.

Sooty Shearwater
Puffinus griseus 15–17in/39–44cm

Identification A dusky, medium-sized
shearwater. Upperparts are uniformly
dusky-brown; underparts similar,
but with a distinctive pale
center to the underwing.
Though a typical shearwater,
the long wings are held slightly
more angled than other species and
flight is more flapping.
Voice Silent at sea.
Habitat Oceans.
Range Breeds only in Southern
Hemisphere. Fall visitor to east coast
(scarce) and west coast (common).
Movements Regular loop migration
into both Pacific and Atlantic Oceans
when not breeding.

Leach's Storm-Petrel
Oceanodroma leucorhoa 7½–8½in/19–22cm

Identification Small, black seabird with
forked tail and bold white rump.
In flight, shows gray coverts extending
across the upper wing. In southern
California white rump is absent.
Feet do not extend beyond tail,
seldom follows ships. Flight
consists of glides and wing flapping.
Voice Various screeches and crooning
at breeding colonies.
Habitat Breeds on remote islands;
winters at sea.
Range Breeds along western coasts and
in the north-east from Labrador to Maine.
Movements Disperses at sea.

Wilson's Storm-Petrel
Oceanites oceanicus 6½–7in/17–18cm

Identification Small, black storm-petrel with white rump, rounded tail and long legs that extend or trail in flight. Gray in wing is similar to Leach's Storm-Petrel, but often follows ships and patters over the surface of the sea. Legs yellow if well seen.
Voice Silent at sea.
Habitat Oceans.
Range Breeds only in southern oceans. Regular off east coast in fall and sometimes quite numerous off Grand Banks.
Migrations Performs huge loop migration in Atlantic.

Brown Pelican
Pelecanus occidentalis 45–54in/114–137cm

Identification Unmistakable, being the only pelican that dives for its food. In summer, adult is silvery-brown with large, dark-brown bill and pouch, creamy neck and chestnut hind-neck and foreneck. In winter the chestnut is lost. Juvenile is brown and whitish, with dark upperparts. In flight, dark body contrasts with pale head. Usually gregarious.
Voice Nestlings produce wide variety of calls; adults silent.
Habitat Sea coasts and lagoons.
Range Breeds along both Pacific and Atlantic coasts and along Gulf Coast.
Movements Largely resident.

American White Pelican

Pelecanus erythrorhynchos 55–70in/140–178cm

Identification Unmistakable huge, white bird with large orange-pink bill and pouch. Adult is all white save for the bill; and for black flight feathers that are particularly apparent in the air. Juvenile has brown crown and bill, but dirty white body. Flies in formation on broad wings.

Voice Usually silent.

Habitat Marshes and lagoons.

Range Breeds in central west Canada southwards to California and Texas.

Movements Winters along coasts and inland in California and Gulf Coast.

Northern Gannet F

Sula bassana 34–38in/86–96cm

Identification Large black and white seabird that gathers at enormous colonies in favored localities. Large, cigar-shaped body with pointed head and tail. Long, stiffish wings with boldly black tips. Flies with series of flaps and long glides, dives from air into sea. Juveniles dark brown, becoming whiter over several years.

Voice Grunts and cackles at colonies.

Habitat Remote islands and stacks; winters at sea.

Range Breeds on islands off Newfoundland, Nova Scotia and in Gulf of St Lawrence.

Movements Disperses over seas as far south as Florida and adjacent Gulf Coast in winter.

Brown Booby
Sula leucogaster 27½–31½in/70–80cm

Identification Closely related and similar to Northern Gannet in shape and behavior. Upperparts, head and neck brown, belly white. Underwing shows white center. Bill, face and large feet, yellow. Basically a tropical species that just reaches North America.
Voice Silent outside breeding season.
Habitat Sea coasts, oceans.
Range Breeds in Mexico on Pacific Coast.
Movements Wanders northwards to coast of southern California and Salton Sea.

Great Cormorant
Phalacrocorax carbo 35–39½in/89–100cm

Identification Largest of the cormorants. Dark bird that swims and dives well and often perches with its wings out to dry. Iridescent green and gold wash over mainly black plumage with, in summer adult, white chin and flank patches. Proportionally larger head and bill and thicker neck than similar species. Juvenile, pale on underparts and best identified by yellow base to bill and by structure.
Voice Various grunts.
Habitat Coastal, sometimes inland lakes.
Range Breeds on Atlantic coast of Canada.
Movements Winters southwards on Atlantic Coast as far as New York area.

Brandt's Cormorant
Phalacrocorax penicillatus
33–35in/84–89cm

Identification Uniformally black
cormorant marked by difficult-to-see
blue throat patch bordered by a
dull creamy patch that is a much
better field mark. Shiny, iridescent
plumage, lacks a crest.
Voice Croaks and grunts while
breeding.
Habitat Coastal, breeds on offshore rocks.
Range Breeds from southern British Columbia to Mexico and
confined to Pacific.
Movements Local dispersal only.

Double-crested Cormorant
Phalacrocorax auritus
30½–36in/77–91cm

Identification All-dark cormorant
with golden sheen on wings like
Great Cormorant. The most common
and widespread member of the family.
Orange-red 'face' is almost the only
distinguishing feature; the double
crests are virtually impossible to see
in the field. Juveniles are buffy below,
brown above and show orange-red on
face.
Voice Grunts while breeding.
Habitat Lakes, rivers and coastal
waters.
Range Breeds throughout most of US and temperate Canada,
though absent from hilly and mountain areas.
Movements Winters along most coasts and inland along southern
river systems.

Olivaceous Cormorant
Phalacrocorax olivaceus
23½–25½in/60–65cm

Identification Small, dark
cormorant with iridescent, olive
plumage and orange-yellow throat
patch bordered by white.
Immature is brown above and
buff below with orange-yellow
throat. Smallest cormorant on
the Atlantic Coast.
Voice Various grunting calls when breeding.
Habitat Marshes, freshwaters and brackish lagoons.
Range Breeds along the coasts of Texas and Louisiana.
Movements Moves southward along Gulf Coast to winter south
of the Mexican border.

Anhinga
Anhinga anhinga 34–36in/86–491cm

Identification Like a large, slim cormorant. Adult male is black
with ragged crest and drooping silver plumes across the back and
wings. The neck is extremely long, the head slim and the bill, long
and dagger-like. The tail is long and broad. In soaring flight, the
extended neck and tail form a 'cross' in the sky. The female has
buffy head and neck.
Voice Various grunting calls.
Habitat Freshwater marshes and overgrown swamps.
Range Breeds in southern states north to North Carolina.
Movements Mostly coastal in winter.

Mute Swan

Cygnus olor
57–63in/145–160cm

Identification A huge, white swimming bird with an extremely long neck. Adults are white with an orange bill and a bare black knob at the base – larger in the male. The wings are often raised over the back. Juvenile is gray-brown becoming white over two or three years.
Voice Silent except for hisses of aggression.
Habitat Ponds and lakes.
Range Introduced from Europe to north-eastern US. Mostly found on Long Island and in New Jersey, New England and Maryland.
Movements Resident, hard weather visitor to coastal bays.

Whistling Swan

Cygnus columbianus
47–58in/119–147cm

Identification Most common and widespread of the swans. Adult is white with long straight neck and black bill. There is usually a

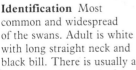

small spot of yellow in front of the eye. Juvenile is gray-brown with dull, pinkish bill.
Voice Goose-like whistled call.
Habitat Marshy tundra ponds in summer; coastal marshes and inland floods in winter.
Range Breeds on western Canadian tundra.
Movements Migrates southwards to winter at traditional sites on Atlantic and Pacific coasts and at a few inland sites in the west.

Canada Goose
Branta canadensis 22–36in/56–92cm

Identification Highly variable in size. Brown and buff body, with long black neck and head, with white area on side extending from chin. Abundant, noisy, well-known.
Voice Loud honking, especially in flight.
Habitat Marshes, lakes.

Range Breeds right across Canada extending southwards through the prairies and Rockies. Small race of Alaska-Yukon known as 'Cackling Goose'.
Movements Migrates throughout Canada and US to winter along Pacific and Atlantic coasts and in temperate US.

Brant
Branta bernicla 23–26in/58–66cm

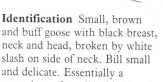

Identification Small, brown and buff goose with black breast, neck and head, broken by white slash on side of neck. Bill small and delicate. Essentially a gregarious, shore-line bird in winter.
This bird breeds right around the northern pole in the tundra zone and has developed several well-marked sub-species. In North America the western sub-species is often treated separately as Black Brant. It differs in having a black belly with pale flanks.
Voice A honking *rank-rank*.
Habitat Tundra in summer, shores and adjacent marshes in winter.
Range High Canadian arctic.
Movements Moves southward to winter along Pacific and Atlantic coasts.

Barnacle Goose
Branta leucopsis
23–27in/58–69cm

Identification Dainty, black
and white goose, with heavily
barred gray upperparts. Breast
and neck black, face white. In flight,
gray upperwing is prominent feature.
Bill is small and black.
Voice Barking yaps.
Habitat Estuaries, grassland near coasts.
Range Arctic breeder that often wanders to North America from
Greenland breeding grounds.
Movements Usually moves southwards to Europe, but some get
caught up with other species and arrive on east coasts.

White-fronted Goose
Anser albifrons
25½–30in/65–76cm

Identification A small, gray
goose that is easily identified.
Basically, barred brown and
buff above, with buffy
underparts marked by bold
black smudges. The base of
the bill and forehead are white,
the bill pink and the legs orange.
Juvenile lacks white forehead and
black belly smudging. Birds
from Greenland have orange
bills.
Voice High-pitched honking.
Habitat Breeds on tundra; winters on grasslands near coast.
Range Western Canadian arctic tundra.
Movements Migrates to west coast and through Central Flyway
to Gulf Coast.

Snow Goose
Anser caerulescens 25–31in/64–79cm

Identification A small goose that is abundant in major breeding and wintering grounds. Adult is pure white with black wing tips and pink bill and legs. Dark phase birds are found in the eastern part of the breeding range and are known as the Blue Goose. They have white head, but blue-brown body and wings.
Voice Nasal, muffled honking.
Habitat Tundra in summer; winters on marshes.
Range From northern Alaska through Canadian arctic to Baffin Island.
Movements Uses all three flyways to winter on Pacific, Atlantic and Gulf Coasts. Also inland in California and elsewhere.

Mallard
Anas platyrhynchos 21½–24½in/55–62cm

Identification Widespread and common duck over much of North America. Male has bottle-green head, white neck ring and brown throat. Upperparts are gray, underparts a pale silver with a black rear end. In flight, there is a blue speculum bordered white. Female is mottled in shades of brown with orange bill.

Voice Loud quacking.
Habitat Ponds, lakes, rivers, marshes, estuaries.
Range Breeds through most of boreal and temperate Canada south through the northern US.
Movements Much of the northern part of the breeding range is abandoned as birds move southwards to winter throughout US.

Black Duck
Anas rubipres 21–24in/53–61cm

Identification A widespread and common, surface-feeding duck in the eastern half of North America. Both sexes resemble female Mallard, but are much darker, with yellow not orange bills. The paler head contrasts with the darker body, the speculum is purple with only the narrowest of white margins. In flight, pale underwing contrasts with dark body.
Voice Loud quacking.
Habitat Ponds, marshes, sea bays.
Range Breeds over eastern half of Canada and north-eastern US.
Movements Winters throughout eastern US to southern Texas.

Northern Pintail
Anas acuta 21–27½in/53–70cm

Identification A slim, elegant duck with extended central tail feathers. Male is delicately colored with a chocolate-brown hood extending to the neck and with various shades of gray on the body terminating in a black and white rear end. The central tail feathers form the pin-tail. Female is mottled in shades of gray-brown. Both sexes have delicate blue bills, long necks and pointed tails.
Voice Quacks.
Habitat Marshes, estuaries.
Range Breeds across eastern half of Canada into Alaska and southward into the eastern US.
Movements Winters on coasts and in southern half of US.

Gadwall
Anas strepera
19−21½in/48−54cm

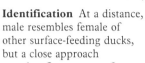

Identification At a distance,
male resembles female of
other surface-feeding ducks,
but a close approach
reveals a fine pattern of
vermiculated grays. Most obvious feature is black rear end and
white speculum. Female similar to female Mallard with orange bill;
but white speculum separates when seen. Smaller, more round-
headed than Mallard.
Voice Quacks.
Habitat Marshes, lakes, estuaries.
Range Breeds in north-western US to California and south-
western Canada.
Movements Migrates through the US to winter on both coasts
and southern half of the country.

American Wigeon
Anas americana
17−19½in/44−50cm

Identification Common duck that forms large flocks at favored
areas. Male (formerly Baldpate) has creamy-gray head with bold
slash of dark green extending from the eye. Underparts are rufous
and separated from the brown upperparts by a bold white lateral
line. Female is more subdued and lacks green eye slash. Both have
small, gray bills. Spends much time grazing. White inner wing only
on male in flight.
Voice Soft whistling.
Habitat Coastal and inland marshes and floods.
Range Breeds from Alaska, through western Canada to north-
western US.
Movements Migrates through whole of US to winter on all coasts
and in southern states.

Northern Shoveler

Anas clypeata 18½–21in/47–53cm

Identification Both sexes have large spatulate bill. Male has green head, chestnut belly and flanks and boldly white breast that is often best feature when resting. Female is like other surface-feeding ducks, but huge bill always apparent. In flight, pale blue inner wing is useful.

Voice Quacking.
Habitat Shallow marshes, ponds, estuaries.
Range Breeds from Alaska, through western Canada to north-western US.
Movements Migrates through US to winter on all coasts and in southern states.

Blue-winged Teal F

Anas discors 14–15½in/36–40cm

Identification Small, Teal-like duck, marked in the male by a slate-blue head with bold white crescent before the eye. Heavily spotted brown on buff below. Female like female Teal, but has pale blue inner wing like the male.

Voice Quiet quacking.
Habitat Ponds, marshes.
Range Breeds over western Canada and US, but not in southern states.
Movements Migrates through US to winter in Florida and along the Gulf Coast.

Cinnamon Teal

Anas cyanoptera 14½–17in/37–43cm

Identification Small duck that looks dark at a distance. Male is, in fact, a deep cinnamon-brown on head and underparts. Upperparts are darkly mottled. Female is mottled in shades of brown. In flight, both show a pale blue forewing like a Blue-winged Teal and pale wing linings contrasting with dark body.
Voice Quacking.
Habitat Marshes, ponds.

Range Breeds over much of western US, extending northwards into adjacent Canada.
Movements Moves southward to winter across Mexican border.

Green-winged Teal

Anas crecca 13½–15in/34–38cm

Identification Common and widespread duck, normally found in flocks. Male has chestnut head broken by green slash through eye, bordered by broken yellow line. Breast is spotted and separated from flanks by vertical white wedge. Rear end is black and cream. Female is like other surface feeding ducks, but with green speculum, bordered white, like male. In flight, white border forms a narrow bar across the wing.
Voice Quacking, whistling.
Habitat Marshes, lakes, estuaries.
Range Breeds in western half of the continent, but not in south-western US.
Movements Migrates throughout US to winter on both coasts and in southern and western states.

Wood Duck

Aix sponsa 17–20in/43–51cm

Identification A woodland duck
with bold, multi-colored plumage.
Male has harlequin patterned
head in purple and
white with red bill
and eye. The upperparts
are an iridescent green,
but with chestnut and blue
in the wing. Female is spotted
below with a gray head broken
by white markings, particularly
around the eye. In flight, the
tail is longer than most other
duck.

Voice Whistling *woo-eek*.
Habitat Woodland ponds and rivers.
Range Resident in far western US and summer visitor to eastern
half of the country northwards into southern Canada.
Movements Eastern birds migrate to winter in Florida and Gulf
Coast.

Fulvous Tree-Duck

Dendrocygna bicolor

18–21in/46–53cm

Identification A gregarious,
upright-standing duck that,
despite its name, only
rarely perches in trees.
Head, neck and
underparts are
barred brown
and black. The long
neck has a bold white slash.
The tail is short, the black
legs long and trail in flight.

Voice Whistling.
Habitat Marshes, ponds.
Range In US along Mexican border to Texas and Louisiana Gulf
Coast.
Movements Summer visitor to North America.

Redhead
Aythya americana
18–22in/46–56cm

Identification A common diving duck. Male has chestnut-red head, black breast and tail and is gray between the two. The head is rounded and the bill gray with a black tip. It resembles the Canvasback, but is darker gray, has a smaller bill and lacks the wedge-shaped head of that bird. Female is similarly shaped, but patterned in gray-browns with pale eye-ring.
Voice Distinct mewing in breeding season.
Habitat Lakes and ponds; estuaries in winter.
Range Breeds among prairies.
Movements Migrates throughout temperate North America to winter on all coasts.

Canvasback
Aythya valisineria 19½–24in/50–61cm

Identification Very similar to
Redhead in plumage
pattern, though male is
paler gray on
body and
female grayer throughout.
Longer neck and
elongated wedge-
shaped head with
all-black bill are
best identification
features

Voice Cooing during breeding season.
Habitat Lakes and marshes; winters along sheltered shorelines and bays.
Range Breeds either side of the US-Canada border in the west, extending further northwards than Redhead.
Movements Migrates throughout US to winter along all coastlines.

Ring-necked Duck
Aythya collaris 15½–18in/40–46cm

Identification Male is a boldly black and white duck, with purple sheen on head and green sheen on breast. The back is black and the flanks gray with a white vertical wedge forwards. It bears a strong resemblance to the scaup, but the dark back, white flank wedge and strongly peaked crown distinguish.

Female is mottled in browns, has a white eye-ring and resembles female Redhead; peaked crown of present species separates at reasonable distance. In flight both sexes show gray wing-bar.

Voice Silent.
Habitat Lakes and ponds.
Range Breeds across southern Canada.
Movements Migrates throughout US to winter near all coasts and throughout the southern states.

Greater Scaup
Aythya marila 15–20in/39–51cm

Identification Marine duck outside the breeding season. Male has black head and breast marked bottle-green, whitish flanks, gray back and black tail. Female is brown with bold white area at base of bill. In flight both show white wing-bar extending across whole of wing. *See* Lesser Scaup.
Voice Soft coos in breeding season.
Habitat Tundra lakes; coastal in winter.
Range Breeds Alaska and neighbouring Canada.
Movements Migrates through whole of North America to winter along all coasts.

Lesser Scaup

Aythya affinis 15–18½in/38–47cm

Identification Similar to Greater Scaup. Head and breast of male washed with purple, not green, sheen; flanks grayer. Female closely resembles female Greater Scaup.

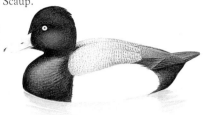

In both sexes the white wing-bar is more obvious on the inner wing, rather than extending across the whole wing as in the Greater Scaup. Additionally the black nail on the bill is tiny.

Voice Cooing in summer.

Habitat Marshes; winters lakes, marshes and estuaries. Far less marine than Greater Scaup.

Range Breeds from Alaska across western Canada to the north-western US.

Movements Migrates throughout to winter on all coasts and inland along river systems and ponds of the south.

Common Goldeneye

Bucephala clangula 15½–19in/40–48cm

Identification Neatly proportioned diving duck with distinct wedge-shaped head. Male has bottle-green head with white spot before the eye. Underparts are white, upperparts black, common separated by an area that is white, striped black. Female has dark chocolate-colored head and is mottled gray above and below. Both sexes show white inner wing in flight. *See* Barrow's Goldeneye.

Voice Quacks in summer.

Habitat Marshes and lakes in boreal forest; lakes and coasts in winter.

Range Northern conifer forests across Canada.

Movements Winters on all coasts and inland throughout the US.

Barrow's Goldeneye
Bucephala islandica 16½–20in/42–51cm

Identification Highly localized relative of Goldeneye. Male similar to Common Goldeneye, but has purple, not green, sheen on head and white crescent, not spot, before eye. Black back and white flanks are separated by black area with white spots – not a white area with black lines. The overall effect is to make this a much darker bird than the Common Goldeneye. Female very similar to female Common Goldeneye. Both sexes have steep forehead.
Voice Various notes when breeding.
Habitat Lakes in forest; coastal in winter.
Range Breeds from Alaska through mountains toWyoming and in northern Labrador.
Movements Winters along west coast to California and in east as far as Long Island. More common in west.

Bufflehead
Bucephala albeola 13–15in/33–38cm

Identification Dainty duck of wooded areas. Male is black above, white below, with black head showing broad white slash extending from eye to nape. Female is browner with white oval behind the eye. Large rounded head and small bill.
Voice Whistles and quacks.
Habitat Pools among conifers; winters on lakes, estuaries.
Range Breeds Alaska and western Canada, extending southwards in Rockies.
Movements Winters on all coasts and throughout ice-free US.

Harlequin Duck
Histrionicus histrionicus 16–17½in/41–45cm

Identification Unique 'torrent' duck that is at home among inland rapids and coastal breakers. Male is gray-blue broken by harlequin pattern of bold white slashes; flanks rust-red. Female brownish, with three pale patches on sides of head. Could be confused with female White-winged and Surf Scoter, but has rounded head and tiny bill.

Voice Croaks in summer.

Habitat Torrents in rivers in summer; rocky coasts in winter.

Range From Alaska southwards through Rockies; and in north eastern Canada.

Movements To the nearest coast in the west, moves southward in the east to New England.

Common Eider
Somateria mollissima 21½–24in/55–61cm

Identification Chunky, heavily built seaduck. Male has white head with black cap and dull green nape. The breast and back are whitish, the underparts black. Female is mottled and barred brown. Both sexes have wedge-shaped head with base of bill extending toward the eye.

Voice Loud cooings when breeding.

Habitat Coasts.

Range Breeds on coasts from British Columbia through Alaska and among the Canadian arctic to Newfoundland, Nova Scotia and Maine.

Movements Winters on Pacific coasts as far south as Vancouver and on Atlantic coasts to Carolina.

King Eier

Somateria spectabilis 21–23in/53–59cm

Identification An arctic breeding duck that is rare in temperate waters. Male is white on breast and black on flanks, back and underparts. The head is a unique pattern of white, blue and orange with an orange bill. Female is mottled brown, but with a much smaller bill than female Common Eider and a more rounded head.

Voice Various croaks.
Habitat Coasts.
Range Breeds arctic coasts.
Movements Winters on ice-free coasts as far south as British Columbia in the west and New England in the east.

Oldsquaw

Clangula hyemalis 16–23in/41–58cm

Identification Attractive sea duck with extended central tail feathers, particularly in the male. Unusual in having distinctive summer and winter plumages. Male, black and white in summer; white and black in winter. Female, blotched brown, with smudgy appearance. Rounded head, short bill and overall shape identify in all plumages.
Voice Yodelling calls in summer.
Habitat Tundra pools; winters along coasts.
Range Canadian arctic in breeding season.
Movements Migrates to winter along both east and west coasts and in Great Lakes.

Common Scoter
Melanitta nigra
18–20in/46–51cm

Identification An all-black seaduck. Male, uniformly black with yellow knob at base of bill. Female, dark brown with paler cheek patches. In mixed flocks at a distance at sea, the pale cheeks of the female are often the only detail visible.
Voice Some croaking in summer.
Habitat Tundra lakes; at sea in winter.
Range Breeds in western Alaska, Newfoundland and Labrador.
Movements Migrates along Pacific coast and across Canada to winter on east coast as far south as Carolina.

White-winged Scoter
Melanitta fusca 21–23in/53–59cm

Identification At any distance male closely resembles other scoter, but has white 'eye' and bold white patch in wing. Female brown, with two pale patches on side of head and similar white in wing.
Voice Croaks in summer.
Habitat Lakes; coastal in winter, but some inland on lakes.
Range Breeds in Alaska in broad band through Manitoba and North Dakota.
Movements Migrates to winter on both east and west coasts and in Great Lakes.

Surf Scoter
Melanitta perspicillata 17–21in/43–53cm

Identification Male
similar to other scoter at
any distance, but close
approach reveals patches
of white on crown and nape, and
boldly-colored orange, red and white bill. Female very closely
resembles female White-winged Scoter with similar pale patches on
sides of head. Both sexes lack white in wing of that bird.
Voice Croaks in summer.
Habitat Tundra in north-western Canada and in Alaska.
Range Breeds Alaska and north-western and north-eastern Canada.
Movements Winters on all coasts.

Ruddy Duck
Oxyura jamaicensis 14–17in/36–43cm

Identification Small, dumpy duck with curious, weight-forward
appearance. Tail often held vertical or hidden in water surface.
In summer, male is rich
chestnut on body, with
white face, black cap
and bright blue bill.
In winter, the colors
are lost and it is clothed
in shades of brown.
Female mottled brown
with distinctive horizontal
stripe across 'face'.

Voice Various croaking calls in summer.
Habitat Marshes and ponds.
Range Breeds through prairies north and south of US-Canada
border, as well as valleys of Rockies. Small population on east
coast.
Movements Migrates throughout US to winter on ice-free waters
near all coasts.

Common Merganser
Mergus merganser
22½–27in/57–69cm

Identification Larger and stouter than Red-breasted Merganser with crest that always points downwards. Male is black above, white below with bottle-green head that extends into rounded hind crest. Female similar to female Red-breasted Merganser, but with rounded, down-pointing crest.
Voice Croaks and cackles in summer.
Habitat Freshwater pools and rivers; mostly freshwater in winter.
Range Breeds through conifer belt of Canada extending southwards in the west.
Movements Migrates southwards to winter in northern and central US.

Red-breasted Merganser
Mergus serrator
20–22in/51–56cm

Identification A slim, sawbill duck with ragged crest. Male has bottle green head, white neck, a speckled brown breast, black and white upperparts and gray flanks. The bill is long, thin and red. Female has rufous head and gray body. In all plumages the spiked crest points horizontally to the rear. Male separated from Common Merganser at any distance by speckled, not white breast.
Voice Various purring and croaking calls while breeding.
Habitat Rivers; in winter on creeks and sea.
Range Breeds among tundra from Alaska through northern Canada.
Movements Migrates through much of US to winter on all three coastlines.

Hooded Merganser

Lophodytes cucullatus 15½−19in/40−48cm

Identification Smallest of the sawbills
with large, erectile crest. Male has
black head with broad, white
wedge extending from
the eye to the nape
in a crest that can
be raised or lowered.
The breast is white with
two narrow bands. Female is
like diminutive female Red-breasted
Merganser, but crest forms a fan rather than two
points. Rather browner above than other female sawbills.
Voice Croaking calls in summer.
Habitat Lakes among woods; winters on lakes near coast.
Range Breeds from coast to coast in a broad area north and south
of the US-Canada border.
Movements Winters near all three coastlines.

Turkey Vulture

Cathartes aura 26−32in/66−81cm

Identification Large, dark bird
of prey. Plumage basically
black with brownish wings.
In the air, the flight feathers
are paler than the wing linings
and the body. Head is bare,
wrinkled and red; gray in
immatures. Soars and glides
on wings held in shallow 'V'.
One of the largest birds of prey
in America.

Voice Silent.
Habitat Open country, roadsides.
Range Breeds virtually throughout US and across Canadian
border in prairies.
Movements Leaves most of northern and central states in winter.

American Black Vulture
Coragyps atratus 23–23½in/58–59cm

Identification All-black bird of prey. The Black Vulture is entirely black, though a silvery sheen shows on the folded wings. The face is bare and black, the bill thin and pointed – not chunky like juvenile Turkey Vulture. In flight the base of the primaries is a bold white. These are gregarious birds that soar on flat wings.
Voice Silent.
Habitat Open country, roadsides and, in the south, shorelines and villages.
Range Resident in southern and eastern states.
Movements May leave northern part of mid-west in winter.

Mississippi Kite
Ictinia mississippiensis 12–14in/30–35cm

Identification Gray above with paler gray head and underparts and a black tail; large flattened head and bold eyes. In the air appears dusky, with bouyant easy flight. Usually gregarious, catching and consuming insects as it flies.
Voice High-pitched whistles.
Habitat Woodland, usually near water.
Range Declining from south and south-eastern states.
Movements Migrates south to South America.

Swallow-tailed Kite

Elanoides forficatus

22–24in/56–61cm

Identification A well-marked bird of prey with easy, masterful flight. Upperparts, wings and tail black, head and underparts white. Flattened head and bold red eye. In the air, the tail is deeply forked and the long pointed wings are black with white linings. Mostly aerial, soaring effortlessly for hours at a time.
Voice Whistles.
Habitat Marshes, thickets, damp woodland.
Range Gulf Coast to Florida and South Carolina.
Movements Migrates to South America.

Northern Goshawk

Accipiter gentilis 19–23in/48–58cm

Identification Large, dashing accipiter mainly confined to northern forests. The smaller male is gray above and streaked on white below. A bold, white eyebrow creates a fierce expression. Female is larger and browner with heavily barred underparts. These magnificent and powerful birds are agile fliers among trees. They soar easily and show a white powder-puff under the tail in diving display.
Voice High-pitched *kee-kee-kee.*
Habitat Conifer forests, but also deciduous forests to the south.
Range Boreal forests of Canada and conifers in Rockies and north-western US. Extending southwards to deciduous forests recently.
Movements Moves southwards as winter visitor to central US.

Cooper's Hawk
Accipiter cooperii

14−20in/35−51cm

Identification Medium-sized accipiter with rounded wings and long tail. Gray above, barred rusty below with rounded tail showing four or five clear bands. Fast and agile flier that soars with series of fast wing beats interupting still-winged gliding.
Voice High-pitched, repetitive *kee-kee-kee.*
Habitat Deciduous woods, sometimes also conifers.
Range Virtually throughout US and into adjacent Canada, but serious decline and disappearance from many areas of US.
Movements Leaves central and northern parts of range in winter.

Sharp-shinned Hawk
Accipiter striatus 10−14in/25−35cm

Identification Smallest of the accipiters. Gray above and barred rusty below. Rounded wings and long-tailed which is square-ended (Cooper's is rounded) and shows four or five clear dark bands. Agile flier in pursuit of small birds.
Voice High-pitched *ka-ka-ka.*
Habitat Conifer and deciduous forests; virtually any woodland or wooded country in winter.
Range From Alaska through boreal Canada to most of the US except the extreme south.
Movements Leaves northern part of range and most of Canada; winters through most of the US.

Northern Harrier

Circus cyaneus 17–20in/43–51cm

Identification A long-winged, long-tailed bird of prey that flaps and glides low over the ground. Male is gray above and white below, with bold white rump band. Female is mottled brown and buff, but same white rump.
Voice Sharp *kee-kee-kee* when breeding.
Habitat Marshes, rough grassland.
Range Breeds over much of Alaska, Canada and the northern US.
Movements Winters virtually throughout US, but only locally in southern Canada.

Rough-legged Hawk

Buteo lagopus
19–24in/48–61cm

Identification A typical buteo, with broad wings and medium-length, white tail, with broad terminal band. Black belly and dark carpal patches are the best field marks. There is much plumage variation and dark birds may show only the characteristic tail. Hovers more than most buteos and soars on flat wings.
Voice Whistling.
Habitat Tundra and thin forests; winters on marshes.
Range Tundra Canada.
Movements Migrates to winter over most of the US except the extreme south. Migrant through temperate Canada.

Ferruginous Hawk

Buteo regalis 22–25in/56–64cm

Identification This is the largest of the buteos and is typically a western bird of arid brush country. Mottled in buffs and browns, but with rufous at bend of wing, on uppertail band and on legs. Rare, dark phase birds are brown with white flight feathers and all-white tail. Pale phase birds are white below, with only rufous patches on carpals, legs and tail.
Voice Raucous cries.
Habitat Open brush, prairies.
Range Breeds either side of the border in western Canada and US.
Movements Canadian birds move southwards to winter in western US and beyond.

Red-tailed Hawk

Buteo jamaicensis 19–25in/48–64cm

Identification The typical phase is brown above and paler below, with a narrow dark band across the belly and a plain rufous tail. A dark phase has brown body and wing linings contrasting with pale primaries. There is much plumage variation including birds with white tails. Young birds have finely-barred, brown tails. Harlan's Hawk is regarded as a phase of this species.

Voice High-pitched *kee-argh*.
Habitat Virtually any open area with adjacent woods – very widespread.
Range Virtually everywhere in North America except open tundra.
Movements Most Canadian birds move south in winter.

Red-shouldered Hawk

Buteo lineatus 15½–24in/40–61cm

Identification Well-marked buteo with rusty 'shoulders'. Upperparts brown, underparts closely barred rufous. In the air the upperwing is clearly banded black and white across the flight feathers, and the tail is equally clearly barred with broad black and narrow white bands. Below, the rusty body and wing linings contrast with pale flight feathers and the tail is barred black and white as above. Longer and more slender wings than Red-tailed Hawk.

Voice Screams.

Habitat Wet woodland.

Range Breeds over most of eastern US and into neighboring Canada. Also in California.

Movements North-eastern part of range abandoned in winter.

Swainson's Hawk ꜰ

Buteo swainsoni

17½–22in/45–56cm

Identification A large buteo that makes the longest of migrations. Brown above and white below, marked by a broad, brown breast band. The tail is white, finely barred, and with a broad subterminal black band. A dark phase is brown below with no obvious breast band, but retains the pale tail pattern. Migrates in great swirling flocks.

Voice Whistle.

Habitat Plains, prairies, open grasslands.

Range From Alaska southwards through most of western and central US.

Movements Migrates south as far as Argentina, but some birds move across the US to winter in Florida.

Broad-winged Hawk

Buteo platypterus 13–15in/33–38cm

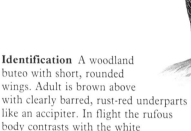

Identification A woodland buteo with short, rounded wings. Adult is brown above with clearly barred, rust-red underparts like an accipiter. In flight the rufous body contrasts with the white wings and neatly banded black and white tail. Migrates in huge flocks.
Voice High-pitched whistle.
Habitat Deciduous forests.
Range Breeds throughout eastern US northwards into Canada as far as the Gulf of St Lawrence.
Movements Winters in South America; abundant over Hawk Mountain.

Harris' Hawk

Parabuteo unicinctus

18–22in/46–56cm

Identification Adult is dark gray on body with rust-red 'shoulders', 'thighs' and, in flight, wing linings. The tail has a white base, a broad black band, is narrowly tipped white and is considerably longer than most other buteos.
Voice A scream.
Habitat Scrub, mesquite, brushland, semi-desert.
Range Penetrates US in south-west.
Movements Resident.

Zone-tailed Hawk
Buteo albonotatus
18½−22½in/47−55cm

Identification A very dark,
virtually black buteo marked by
black and white barred flight
feathers, from below, and by a
black and white barred tail.
There are two or three clear-cut
black bands on the tail − the
similar, but rarer, Black Hawk,
has only one broad, black tail
band.
Voice Loud whistles.
Habitat Scrub and semi-desert.
Range Arizona, New Mexico
and western Texas.
Movements May move across
border into Mexico.

Golden Eagle
Aquila chrysaetos
30−35½in/76−90cm

Identification Huge,
magnificient eagle which could
be confused only with Bald Eagle
in juvenile plumage. Adult is brown
above and below, with wash of
'gold' on crown and nape. Juvenile
and immatures have white base to
tail and white bar along underwing.
Soars on huge flat wings, glides
over hillsides. Eagles have large
prominent heads compared with
buteos.
Voice Quiet mewing − mostly silent.
Habitat Tundra, mountains.
Range Northern Canada and western US.
Movements Northern birds move southwards over much US.

Bald Eagle
Haliaeetus leucocephalus
30–43in/76–109cm

Identification Large brown eagle with white head and neck and white tail. Juveniles are all brown, but feathers of tail usually show white bases at centers. Large yellow bill.
Voice Loud yelping.
Habitat Coasts, rivers, lakes.
Range Once widespread now confined to Alaska, northern Canada, some remote areas of US, and Florida.
Movements Winters along Pacific coast and in eastern half of US.

Osprey F
Pandion haliaetus
21–24½in/53–62cm

Identification Lightly-built, gray and white bird of prey that is a pure 'fisherman'. Gray-brown above with small white head marked by black eyestripe. Underparts white. In flight, shows black barring across white underwing and bold, black carpal patches. The wings are long and narrow and held arched, like a gull. Hovers and plunges to catch prey.
Voice High-pitched whistles.
Habitat Shorelines, estuaries, lakes, rivers.
Range Breeds over much of North America, though absent from central US.
Movements Winters California, Florida and southwards.

Gyr Falcon

Falco rusticolus 20–25in/51–64cm

Identification A bird of the high arctic that only rarely wanders to US. Three distinct color phases occur, as well as intermediate plumages. Long, pointed wings, shortish tail and streamline shape pick out as a falcon. Most spectacular is white phase which is white, lightly speckled black. A gray phase is very pale, but more heavily speckled black, especially above. A dark phase is slate-gray above and heavily speckled below. The latter resembles a Peregrine, but lacks a prominent moustache.

Voice Slow *ka-ka-ka*.

Habitat Tundra, cliffs; in winter mainly coastal.

Range Alaskan and Canadian tundra including the archipelago.

Movements Irregular movements south to just beyond US border.

Prairie Falcon

Falco mexicanus 17–20in/43–51cm

Identification Brown falcon of the west, that is common where found. Upperparts, brown, edged buffy to produce a 'scaled' appearance. Underparts, white streaked brown. Head shows narrow moustachial streak that is repeated toward rear of head. Pale crown. In flight, shows narrow black axillaries – armpits.

Voice Shrill *kree-kree-kree*.

Habitat Mountains, prairies.

Range The west from British Columbia to Mexico.

Movements Moves southward from northern half of North American range.

Peregrine Falcon

Falco peregrinus 15–18½in/38–48cm

Identification Medium-sized,
powerful falcon. Slate-gray
above, white below,
closely barred black.
The black moustache
against a white 'face' is
a prominent field mark.
The wings are long and
angular, the tail relatively
short. Juvenile is brown and
streaked, rather than barred,
below.
Voice Loud *kek-kek-kek*.
Habitat Cliffs on coasts,
rivers, mountains.
Range Virtually extirpated
by pesticide poisoning. Confined
to far north – some reintroductions.
Movements Northern birds migrate to winter through Canada
and northern states.

Merlin

Falco columbarious

10½–12½in/27–32cm

Identification Small, stocky
falcon that takes mainly small
birds. Male is slate-gray above
with striped breast and only a
hint of a moustachial streak.
Female is brown and similarly
marked. Flies low over ground,
perches openly at dawn and
dusk waiting to hunt.
Voice *Ki-ki-ki* when breeding.
Habitat Open tundra, moors,
mountains; plus coasts in winter.
Range Breeds from Alaska across Canada and southwards through
the Rockies.
Movements Migrates southwards to western, eastern and
southern states.

American Kestrel
Falco sparverius
9–11in/23–28cm

Identification A dainty, well-marked falcon, common over much of North America. Male has rusty, black-barred back with dark blue inner wings. The head is boldly marked with patches of rust, white and black. The rusty tail is long and banded black at tip. Female is browner, with more barring and has only a rudimentary head pattern. Frequently hovers.
Voice High-pitched *kee-kee-kee*.
Habitat Open country.
Range Breeds everywhere except tundra.
Movements Canadian and mountain birds move southwards.

Aplomado Falcon
Falco femoralis
15–18in/38–46cm

Identification Medium-sized falcon of the extreme south. Adult is well marked with slate-gray upperparts, black belly and rusty legs and undertail. The white breast stands out at a distance and a closer approach reveals pale eyebrow. The long tail is banded black and white.
Voice Repeated *ka-ka-ka*.
Habitat Desert and dry grassland.
Range Rare along Mexican border.
Movements Wanders in breeding area.

Common Turkey

Meleagris gallopavo

36–48in/91–122cm

Identification Large ground bird with blue and red head wattles, iridescent black plumage and large tail, fanned in display.
Voice Loud gobbling.
Habitat Woodland clearings, scrub.
Range Scattered through US, once more widespread.
Movements Resident.

Spruce Grouse

Dendragapus canadensis

15–17in/38–43cm

Identification Common grouse of conifer forests. Male has black chin enclosed by white border and black on breast and central belly. There is a red wattle above the eye. Female heavily barred, but with black tail tipped rufous.
Voice Low-pitched booming.
Habitat Conifer forests.
Range Boreal zone from Alaska to Nova Scotia.
Movements Resident.

Ruffed Grouse

Bonasa umbellus 16–19in/41–48cm

Identification Secretive bird of forest edges. There are two color phases: red and gray. 'Red' birds are rufous above with brown barring below. The tail is large and heavily banded rust and black. 'Gray' birds are gray rather than rusty. Both phases have a dark mark on the side of the neck and fan their tail in flight and in display on a hollow log.
Voice Drumming sound produced by beating wings.
Habitat Forests, both deciduous and conifer.
Range The boreal zone extending southwards in Rockies and Appalachians and elsewhere.
Movements Resident.

Sharp-tailed Grouse

Tympanuchus phasianellus 15–20in/38–51cm

Identification Grassland grouse. Rather dully colored in shades of buff and brown in both sexes. Tail is pointed, larger in the male, and is fanned in display, when male shows violet patch on neck.
Voice Cooing in courtship.
Habitat Clearings in forest, open country.
Range Breeds from Alaska through north, west and central Canada as far east as Hudson's Bay and southwards into the prairies.
Movements Resident.

Greater Prairie Chicken

Tympanuchus cupido 15½–18in/40–46cm

Identification Once widespread, now decidedly rare bird of open plains. Lesser Prairie Chicken, of arid south-west, is regarded as a sub-species, not a separate species. Heavily barred brown and black bird with elaborate display using yellow or pink neck sacs and extended crest. Square cut, black tail.
Voice Booming.
Habitat Prairies.
Range Remnants of former range in Mid-West.
Movements Resident.

Willow Ptarmigan

Lagopus lagopus 11–17in/28–43cm

Identification Stocky grouse of open country. Male is rich rufous, with red comb and white wings and feet. In winter, whole plumage becomes white, when confusion with closely-related Rock Ptarmigan is likely.
Voice Crowing *koc-koc-koc*.
Habitat Tundra, open moors.
Range Alaska, northernmost Canada to Newfoundland.
Movements Some birds move south a short distance in winter.

Rock Ptarmigan

Lagopus mutus 13–14in/33–36cm

Identification Similar to Willow
Ptarmigan, but mottled gray rather than
red. Also white in winter, but dark mark
between bill and eye creates an 'angry'
expression.
Voice A rolling *karr*.
Habitat Found at higher altitudes
and higher latitudes than
Willow Ptarmigan; tundra and mountain
tops.
Range Extreme north Canada and
archipelago from Alaska to
Newfoundland.
Movements Some southward
movement in winter.

Scaled Quail

Callipepla squamata 10–12in/25–30cm

Identification A distinctive western quail with a pale crest that
gives it its country name of 'cotton-top'. Gray-brown above, rufous
below and heavily 'scaled' over most of foreparts.
Gregarious, runs rather than flies.
Voice A twanging *be-cos, be-cos*.
Habitat Semi-desert.
Range South-west US.
Movements Resident.

Northern Bobwhite
Colinus virginianus
8–11in/20–28cm

Identification Virtually the
only small gamebird that is at
all common in the eastern US.
Male is brown above, scaled
white below, with distinctive
white face enclosed by black.
Female is similar, but has
creamy face and less black.
Best located by call.
Voice Distinctive *bob-white*.
Habitat Grasslands, farms.
Range Virtually the eastern half of the US to foothills of Rocky
Mountain system. Introduced in the west.
Movements Resident.

Common Pheasant
Phasianus colchicus
20½–35½in/52–90cm

Identification Large colorful
gamebird introduced from Europe.
Male boldly colored in rich browns
and golds, liberally spotted and
barred in black and white. Blue
head with bare red area around
eye, often white neck-ring.
Female subdued shades of
brown and buff, with paler
area around eye. Both sexes
have long, pointed tails.
Voice Deep, resonant crowing.
Habitat Fields, thickets, woodland edges.
Range Widespread across northern US and
southern Canada.
Movements Resident.

Gray Partridge

Perdix perdix 11½–12½in/29–32cm

Identification Chunky gamebird with orange face, brown streaked upperparts and gray breast. Underparts show smudgy chestnut 'horseshoe'. Gregarious bird of open areas.
Voice A fast *krikri-kri-kri-krikri*.
Habitat Fields, grasslands.
Range Either side of US-Canada border right across the continent. Introduced from Europe.
Movements Resident.

Common Egret

Egretta alba 35–41in/89–104cm

Great White Egret

Identification Largest, all-white egret marked by large yellow bill and dark legs. Neck mostly held in distinctly kinked manner when at rest. The white form of the Great Blue Heron found in Florida is larger and has gray-green legs.
Voice Croaks.
Habitat Marshes, pools, estuaries.
Range Breeds over much of the US except the grassland and mountain interior.
Movements Moves southward to winter on south-eastern, Gulf and southern Pacific coasts.

Snowy Egret F
Egretta thula 20–27in/51–68cm

Identification Slim, elegant egret
with white plumage, black bill,
black legs and yellow feet.
When feeding in mud the
feet may appear black, even
in flight afterwards. Young Little
Blue Heron is also white, but has
heavier gray bill and paler legs.
Voice Mostly silent.
Habitat Marshes, lake margins,
estuaries.
Range Widespread over western,
eastern and southern states.
Movements Migrates southward in winter to South America,
though some overwinter in California and from Florida north to
South Carolina.

Cattle Egret
Bubulcus ibis 19–21in/48–53cm

Identification Small, robust, white
egret that associates with domestic
animals and agricultural
machinery. Neck mostly
held tucked into shoulders;
upright walking stance;
yellow bill and black legs.
In breeding season bill
becomes orange, legs become
pink and there is a warm wash
of buff on head, back and breast.
Voice Usually silent.
Habitat Marshes, grasslands, arable.
Range Colonist this century from Old World. Has spread
northwards through southern and eastern states as far as New
England. Has been recorded in eastern Canada.
Movements Largely resident.

Great Blue Heron
Ardea herodias
39–52in/99–132cm

Identification Large, mainly
gray heron with white head
marked by fine black crest.
Pale, streaked foreneck. Flies
on huge arched, dark wings
with neck tucked back in
'shoulders'.
Voice Harsh squawks.
Habitat Ponds, lakes, marshes,
estuaries.
Range Widespread resident over
most of temperate North America.
Movements Northern birds move
southwards in winter.

Reddish Egret F
Egretta rufescens 27½–31½in/70–80cm

Identification Dark egret usually found on salty or brackish
lagoons. Slate-gray body, with bold rusty head, neck and breast that
is held fluffed-up to produce an ill-kempt appearance. The legs are
black, the bill dark pink, with a black tip. A white phase also
occurs, but bill and legs are colored as normal birds. Active feeder.
Voice Croaks.
Habitat Saline lagoons, estuaries.
Range Florida and Texas coastlines.
Movements Resident.

Louisiana Heron F

Egretta tricolor 25–30in/63–76cm

Identification A slate-blue heron,
with white underparts and rufous plumes at
the base of the neck and on the back.
The foreneck is white, streaked and
with a rufous wash. The dagger-like
bill is black, the legs dull yellow.
Always appears more slender and
longer necked than other herons
and egrets.
Voice Various croaking calls.
Habitat Marshes, mangrove
swamps, estuaries, backwaters.
Range From Gulf Coast to Florida northwards to New England.
Movements Resident through most of range.

Little Blue Heron F

Egretta caerulea 25–30in/63–76cm

Identification Adult is dark, slate-gray with maroon neck. The
bill is gray tipped black, the legs gray. It thus bears a superficial
resemblance to the larger Reddish Egret. Common in areas of
south. Young birds are white – beware confusion with egrets.
Voice Croaks while breeding.
Habitat Marshes, lagoons,
often near coast.
Range Breeds along Gulf
Coast and northward up
the major river systems.
Also in Florida and along
the Atlantic Coast to New
England.
Movements Becomes essentially
coastal in winter.

Green Heron F
Butorides striatus
15–22in/38–56cm

Identification Small, bittern-like heron of dense thickets and
aquatic vegetation. Adult has chestnut face, neck and breast with
dark green upperparts. There is a black crest and it has reddish
legs. Usually seen flying on rounded wings between one patch of
cover and another like dark Least Bittern.
Voice Sharp croaks.
Habitat Marshes and lake margins with dense vegetation.
Range Breeds in western and eastern states, absent from prairies
and Rockies.
Movements Winters southern California and Florida, otherwise
migratory from remainder of range.

Black-crowned Night Heron
Nycticorax nycticorax 23–28in/58–71cm

Identification A crepuscular heron
most active at dawn and dusk.
Always holds itself hunched up,
disguising its length of neck.
Adult has black crown and back,
gray wings and white underparts.
The bill is decidedly chunky,
the legs a yellow-orange.
Immatures are streaked in a
gray-buff. In flight, the chunky
effect is enforced.
Voice Various croaks.
Habitat Flooded thickets, riversides.
Range Breeds over much of US northwards into southern Canada.
Movements Winters in west and east, including Mississippi River
system.

Yellow-crowned Night Heron F

Nycticorax violaceus 22–27in/56–68cm

Identification Adult is gray on neck and underparts with boldly black and white upperparts and a unique striped head. A yellow crest extends behind crown. The black bill is chunky. Stands upright and hunts both by day and night. Immature closely resembles young Black-crowned Night Heron.

Voice Various barking notes.

Habitat Marshes and thickets.

Range Breeds along Gulf and Atlantic coasts and inland in Mississippi basin.

Movements Winters along Gulf Coast and in Florida.

American Bittern

Botaurus lentiginosus
23–34in/58–86cm

Identification Large, round-winged heron that skulks among reeds beds and is usually seen briefly in flight. Whole plumage streaked in buffs and browns with a dark cap and broad dark moustachial streak. Bill is large and yellow, legs green. When caught in open, tries to merge with imaginary marsh-type vegetation.

Voice A booming *onk-a-sonk*.

Habitat Marshes.

Range Breeds across southern Canada and much of US.

Movements Leaves northern and central parts of range in winter.

Least Bittern F

Ixobrychus exilis 11−14in/28−35cm

Identification Very small heron that clings to tops of bushes or reeds, but spends most of its time inside deep cover. Male has black crown and back with bold, warm, buffy wing patches, that are particularly obvious in flight. Female and immature similar, but more dully colored.

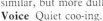

Voice Quiet coo-ing.
Habitat Marshes, reed-beds.
Range Absent from prairies and mountains, otherwise widely spread across US.
Movements Migratory wintering only in Florida, southern Texas and southern California.

American Wood Stork F

Mycteria americana

40−44in/102−112cm

Identification Still widely called 'Wood Ibis'. Large white bird with bare, black head and upper neck, and long, thick decurving black bill. The long legs trail prominently in flight when the white body and wing linings contrast with the flight feathers. Soars like other storks and nests in large colonies.
Voice Croaks when breeding.
Habitat Marshes with trees.
Range Breeds from Gulf Coast to Florida and north to South Carolina.
Movements Winters Florida.

White-faced Glossy Ibis
Plegadis chihi
22–25in/56–63cm

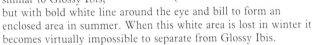

Identification A bronzy-purple,
glossy-plumaged bird, with long
legs, long neck and long
decurved bill. Very
similar to Glossy Ibis,
but with bold white line around the eye and bill to form an
enclosed area in summer. When this white area is lost in winter it
becomes virtually impossible to separate from Glossy Ibis.
Voice Quacking calls.
Habitat Marshes with thickets and reeds.
Range From California inland to Idaho and along Texas and
Louisiana coasts.
Movements Winters Mexico and southern California.

Glossy Ibis F
Plegadis falcinellus 22–25in/56–63cm
Identification Glossy-purple and bronze bird with long legs and
long decurved bill. Very similar to White-faced Ibis, especially in
winter.
Voice Croaks and grunts.
Habitat Marshes with thickets and reeds.

Range Expanding northwards
to Great Lakes and westwards to
Texas from stronghold in Florida.
Probably colonized New World
only a hundred years ago or so as,
equally probably, did the White-faced
Ibis hundreds of years earlier.
Movements Mostly migrates
to Florida to winter.

White Ibis F

Eudocimus albus 23–27in/58–68cm

Identification Large, all-white bird
marked by black wing tips; red
face, decurved red bill, red legs.
Juvenile is brown above, white
below with brown neck. Like other
ibises, flies with neck extended.
Voice Various grunting calls.
Habitat Marshes, lagoons, estuaries.
Range Breeds along Gulf Coast to Florida, north to South
Carolina.
Movements Mostly resident.

Roseate Spoonbill F

Platalea ajaja 30–32in/76–81cm

Identification Large pink bird
with white neck and large, spatulate
gray bill. Immature is white, with
yellow bill and legs. Flies ibis-like with
neck extended. Side-to-side sweeping of
bill facilitates picking it out at great range.
Voice Croaks.
Habitat Mangrove swamps.
Range Florida and Texas
coasts, but very local.
Movements Resident.

Whooping Crane

Grus americana 45–50in/114–127cm

Identification Spectacular, large, white waterbird that may still recover from the verge of extinction. Whole plumage is white save for black wing tips. Cascading 'tail' plumes are actually extended tertial wing feathers. Head with black through eye and bright red crown.
Voice Rolling, trumpeting calls.
Habitat Breeds in bogs; winters in marshes.
Range Breeds only in Wood Buffalo National Park, Canada, though a separate population has been established artificially in recent years at Gray's Lake Refuge, Idaho.
Movements Migrates south to winter at Aransas National Wildlife Refuge, Texas. New population winters New Mexico.

Sandhill Crane F

Grus canadensis

34–48in/86–122cm

Identification Gray crane, with droopy gray 'tail' and red topped crown. Like other cranes, flies with neck extended.
Voice Loud rolling rattle.
Habitat Marshes, ponds and tundra.
Range Breeds over large areas of Canadian and Alaskan tundra as well as on prairies westwards to Pacific coast. Also in Florida.
Movements Spectacular migrations southward to Mexico, California and Texas. Resident Florida.

Limpkin F
Aramus guarauna 25–28in/64–71cm

Identification Superficial
resemblance to a curlew.
A medium-sized waterbird with brown
plumage spotted white. Long legs and
heavy decurved bill. Labored flight
with neck extended.
Voice Loud *krrow*.
Habitat Marshes
with pomacea snails.
Range Florida and adjacent Georgia.
Movements Resident.

Virginia Rail F
Rallus limicola
9–11in/23–28cm

Identification Colorful, long-billed rail. Upperparts streaked
black and brown, underparts warm rust with undertail black, finely
barred white. Legs reddish; bill reddish, slightly decurved.
Immature is dusky, streaked gray and black, with black and white
barred undertail. Skulking and seldom seen.
Voice Characteristic *kickit-kickit-kickit*.
Habitat Marshes with dense vegetation.
Range Breeds right across US, save for southern states,
northwards into Canada.
Movements Winters Pacific coast, Florida and Gulf and Atlantic
coasts.

Sora Rail ⌐

Porzana carolina 8–10in/20–25cm

Identification Common but secretive rail. Adult is streaked brown above and plain gray below, with black and white striped undertail. A dark crown, black 'face' and central breast make identification easy, if seen. Bill and legs yellow. Immature has dusky face, yellow bill, green legs.
Voice A pleasant, descending trill.
Habitat Marshes.
Range Throughout northern US and southern Canada.
Movements Winters California, Gulf and Atlantic coasts and Florida. Most birds leave North America.

Yellow Rail ⌐

Coturnicops noveboracensis 6–8in/15–20cm

Identification Small buff and brown rail marked by yellow legs and bill and smudgy, dark mark through eye. Banded on undertail coverts. Shows bold white patch on trailing edge of inner wing when flushed.
Voice Click notes in series of twos and threes — like tapping two stones together.
Habitat Floods, damp grasslands.

Range Breeds across much of central and eastern Canada, as well as in adjacent areas across the US border.
Movements Winters California, Gulf and Atlantic coasts and Florida.

Black Rail F
Laterallus jamaicensis 5–6in/13–15cm

Identification Tiny black rail
that mainly frequents brackish
coastal marshes. Foreparts
blue-black; back and hindparts
black with fine white vertical
bars. Patch of chestnut at top
of back. Bill short and conical.
Very difficult to see.
Voice High pitched
kic-ki-doo, the last note being
quieter and lower pitched.
Habitat Salt, brackish and
sometimes fresh marshes.
Range Breeds both Pacific
and Atlantic coasts and in
some places inland.
Movements Winters Florida and Gulf Coast.

Clapper Rail
Rallus longirostris 14–15½in/35–40cm

Identification A large pale rail,
similar to King Rail, but largely
confined to salt marshes.
Upperparts gray-brown, lightly
streaked; underparts gray on
breast, banded gray and white
on flanks and undertail. Bill
long and yellowish, legs pinkish.
Voice Loud *kek-kek-kek-kek*.
Habitat Saltmarsh.
Range Most coasts of US,
though less continuous along
rocky Pacific.
Movements Resident.

King Rail F
Rallus elegans
15−19in/38−48cm

Identification Freshwater
equivalent of Clapper Rail.
Slightly larger and much
more clearly marked with
warm rufous breast being
the major feature.
Upperparts streaked brown
and black, undertail and flanks
finely barred black and white.
Voice Deep *kep-kep-kep* similar to Clapper Rail, but more musical.
Habitat Fresh marshes.
Range Breeds over eastern half of US.
Movements Most birds migrate, but some winter along Atlantic
and Gulf coasts, in Florida and in the Mississippi basin.

Common Gallinule
Gallinula chloropus 12−14in/31−35cm

Identification Medium-sized waterbird that swims well and is
often confiding, even tame. Back is dark brown separated from the
black underparts by a bold white, flank slash. The undertail is
white and frequently cocked when walking. The remaining
plumage is black with a bold, red, frontal shield. The legs are
green-yellow, with long toes; the bill red, tipped yellow.
Voice Loud *currick*.
Habitat Pond and lake margins.
Range Breeds over most of eastern US and in Pacific Coast area.
Movements Migrates southwards to Gulf and Atlantic coasts.

American Purple Gallinule

Porphyrula martinica 11–13in/28–33cm

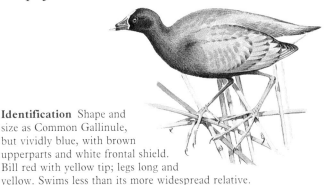

Identification Shape and
size as Common Gallinule,
but vividly blue, with brown
upperparts and white frontal shield.
Bill red with yellow tip; legs long and
yellow. Swims less than its more widespread relative.
Voice Harsh cackling.
Habitat Marshes with plentiful vegetation.
Range Florida, Gulf Coast and adjacent Atlantic Coasts.
Movements Winters along Gulf Coast and in Florida.

American Coot

Fulica americana 14–15in/35–39cm

Identification All-black waterbird that spends much time
swimming. Runs over water to avoid danger and may then show
white trailing edge to the wing. Otherwise white bill and frontal
shield, plus white outer feathers of undertail coverts are the best
field marks.
Voice Sharp *kuk-kuk-kuk.*
Habitat Ponds, lakes, coastal bays.
Range Breeds over most of temperate North America northwards
into the Canadian prairies.
Movements Leaves interior in winter.

American Oystercatcher
Haematopus palliatus
17−21in/43−53cm

Identification Large, chunky, pied shorebird, black above and white below. Shows bold, white wing-bar in flight. Long, thick bill is red; strong legs are pink.
Voice Loud *kleep*.
Habitat Mud flats, shorelines.
Range Breeds from New England southwards along Atlantic Coast and at a few spots on the Gulf Coast.
Movements Leaves northern coasts in winter.

American Avocet
Recurvirostra americana
16−20in/41−51cm

Identification Slim, elegant shorebird with long blue legs and black recurved bill. Feeds with side-to-side motion, sifting soft mud. Black and white plumage with rusty wash on head and neck.

Voice Loud *kleep*.
Habitat Fresh and saline lakes.
Range Breeds western half of US northwards into Canada.
Movements Moves to coasts in winter.

Black-winged Stilt
Himantopus himantopus
13–16in/33–41cm

Identification Often called
Black-necked Stilt, but now
regarded as conspecific with
Old World birds.
Extremely long-legged
wader; black above, white
below with long neck and
needle-like bill. Pink
legs trail in flight.
Voice Loud repeated
keep-keep.
Habitat Fresh and saline
pools and shallow marshes.
Range Western US and,
in the south, along the
Gulf Coast to Florida.
Movement Migrant, but
winters California.

Mountain Plover
Charadrius montanus
8–9½in/20–24cm

Identification Brown plover
with white underparts in
summer. Sandy smudges
at sides of breast, black
crown, white forehead and
eyebrow are main features. In winter, face and breast are washed
sandy. White wing-bar and tail margins in flight.
Voice *Krrr* in flight.
Habitat Grassy plains at altitude.
Range Breeds through eastern foothills of Rockies.
Movements Moves southward to winter, but regular as far north
as California.

American Golden Plover
Pluvialis dominica 9½–11in/24–28cm

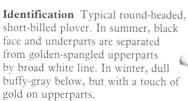

Identification Typical round-headed,
short-billed plover. In summer, black
face and underparts are separated
from golden-spangled upperparts
by broad white line. In winter, dull
buffy-gray below, but with a touch of
gold on upperparts.
Voice Fast *teu-ee*.
Habitat Tundra, grassland.
Range Breeds Alaskan and Canadian tundra to Baffin Island.
Movements Migrates southwards over Atlantic to winter in South
America. Returns in spring through Central Flyway.

Black-bellied Plover
Pluvialis squatarola
11–12in/28–31cm

Identification Similar to
golden plovers, but in all
plumages spangled black
and white above. In
summer 'face' and belly are
black, bordered by white line. In winter, underparts mottled gray.
Shows white wing bar and black axillaries (arm pits) in flight.
Voice Whistled *tlee-oo-ee*.
Habitat Tundra; in winter, estuaries and shorelines.
Range Breeds far northern Alaska and Canada.
Movements Migrates to winter all coasts as far north as
Washington and New England.

Piping Plover

Charadrius melodus 6–6½in/15–17cm

Identification Small sandy plover with narrow, black breast band, wider at side of neck in summer. In winter, only smudge at side of neck remains. Yellow legs separate from similar Snowy Plover. Broad wing-bar and white rump show in flight.
Voice Whistling *peep-lo*.
Habitat Sandy wastes.
Range From prairies through Great Lakes to Atlantic Coast southward to Virginia.
Movements Migrates to winter on Atlantic and Gulf coasts.

Snowy Plover

Charadrius alexandrinus

6–6½in/15–17cm

Identification Small sandy plover marked in summer and winter by dark marks at sides of breast. Immature shows no more than a smudge. Legs black. Wing-bar and white, outer tail show in flight.
Voice *Wit-wit-wit*.
Habitat Sandy wastes and margins of saline and fresh marshes, open shorelines.
Range Breeds locally throughout the west, and along the Pacific Coast.
Movements Migrates southward and to the Pacific Coast to winter.

Semipalmated Plover
Charadrius semipalmatus 6½–8in/17–20cm

Identification Common along
shorelines. Brown above and white
below marked by neat head pattern
of black and white, and bold, black
breast band. Orange bill tipped
black; orange or yellowish
legs.
Voice Pleasant *chur-lee.*
Habitat Breeds tundra; winters, sandy shores and estuaries.
Range Alaskan and Canadian tundra.
Movements Migrates to winter in California and along Atlantic
and Gulf coasts.

Wilson's Plover ✕
Charadrius wilsonia 6½–8in/17–20cm

Identification Similar to Semipalmated Plover but with more
prominent white eyebrow and black eye stripe, and much broader
breast band. Bill is black and heavy, the legs a dull pink. Bill size,
accentuated by sloping forehead, is best field mark.

Voice *Quit-quit.*
Habitat Sandy and muddy shorelines.
Range Gulf and Atlantic coasts to Virginia.
Movements Winters Florida and Gulf Coast.

Killdeer
Charadrius vociferus
9–11in/23–28cm

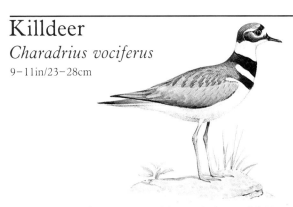

Identification Common and widespread plover of fields and grasslands. Easily picked out by black face pattern and double, black breast bands. Rusty rump and pointed tail most visible in flight.
Voice *Kill-dee*, repeated.
Habitat Fields and grasslands.
Range Breeds throughout US and temperate Canada.
Movements Leaves northern and central parts of range in winter.

Long-billed Curlew
Numenius americanus 20–26in/51–66cm

Identification Unmistakable, large, brown shorebird with huge, decurved bill. Young birds have shorter bills. Cinnamon underwing is diagnostic.
Voice Clear *coo-lee*.
Habitat Prairies in summer; winters on estuaries, shorelines.
Range Western states from high plateaus to upland prairies extending northwards into Canada and south to Texas.
Movements Migrates south to western Gulf Coast and California.

Whimbrel F

Numenius phaeopus 15–17in/39–43cm

Identification Large shorebird with striped crown and longish decurved bill. Similar to Long-billed Curlew, but smaller, shorter bill curves more toward the tip. Rare Bristle-thighed Curlew of west Alaska is very similar, but has rusty rump.

Voice Seven high pitched whistles form a trill.

Habitat Tundra, shorelines and marshes in winter.

Range Breeds coastal Alaska and Canadian arctic.
Movements Migrates mostly along coasts to winter in California and Florida.

Marbled Godwit

Limosa fedoa
16–20in/41–51cm

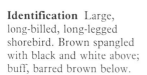

Identification Large, long-billed, long-legged shorebird. Brown spangled with black and white above; buff, barred brown below. Long pinkish bill, tipped black and slightly uptilted. Legs gray, trail in flight. No prominent marks in flight. *See* Hudsonian Godwit.

Voice *Kar-rack*.

Habitat Grasslands; in winter, near coasts or along shorelines.
Range Prairies of US-Canada border.
Movements Migrates southward to winter in California and Gulf Coast.

Hudsonian Godwit
Limosa haemastica
14–15in/36–39cm

Identitication Smaller than
Marbled Godwit and marked at all
times by black and white rump and tail pattern, and white wing-
bar. In summer, chestnut breast is closely barred black. In winter,
is brown above and buff below.
Voice *Quit-quit.*
Habitat High arctic tundra, estuaries in winter.
Range Northernmost Canada to western shores of Hudson's Bay.
Movements Passes out over Atlantic on way to South American
wintering grounds. Returns via Central Flyway.

Upland Sandpiper
Bartramia longicauda
11–12½in/28–32cm

Identification A shorebird that
is most at home on grassland.
Streaked brown and black above,
streaked and arrowed brown
below, with contrasting white
belly. Long yellow legs, long
thin neck with curiously
emaciated look to head. Medium-length, thin bill and long,
wedge-shaped tail. The shape, buffy coloration and habitat
preference make this an easily identified bird.
Voice *Quip-ip-ip-ip.*
Habitat Grasslands.
Range From Alaska through prairies eastwards to the Great Lakes,
the mid-west and Maine.
Movements Leaves North America to winter.

Buff-breasted Sandpiper
Tryngites subruficollis 7½– 8½in/19–21cm

Identification Uniformly warm-buff underparts and plain face pick this bird out easily. Upperparts darkly streaked, thin bill, yellow legs.
Voice *Preeet.*
Habitat Breeds tundra, passage and winter on short-grass meadows and fields.
Range Breeds only north Canadian arctic west of Hudson's Bay to north-east Alaska.
Movements Fall, migrant on east coast; winters Argentina.

Solitary Sandpiper
Tringa solitaria
8–8½in/20–22cm

Identification A bird of ponds and streams rather than open marshes and estuaries. Taller, slimmer and more elegant than Spotted Sandpiper. Upperparts very dark, liberally spotted white. Streaked on sides of neck, breast, and lightly barred on flanks. Long neck, rounded head, medium length thin bill. Legs long and black, trail beyond tail in flight. Dark rump, black and white barred tail and uniform dark wings show in flight. Several other dark sandpipers have white rump.
Voice *Weet-weet-weet.*
Habitat Ponds, streams, breeds on boggy pools.
Range Mainly boreal zone from Alaska across Canada.
Movements Winters southwards in Central and South America.

Spotted Sandpiper ♀
Actitis macularia
7½in/19cm

Identification Brown above, white below, evenly spotted with black in summer. In winter, underparts are white and best field mark is wedge of white between breast and wing. Bobs body continuously, flies low on jerky wings.
Voice High-pitched *weet-weet*.
Habitat Running streams, ponds, lakesides, marshes.
Range Breeds over most of North America except extreme tundra and all southern US.
Movements Winters Florida, Texas and California southwards.

Willet
Catoptrophorus semipalmatus 14–17in/36–43cm

Identification A large gray shorebird that is heavily barred and streaked in summer, but gray and white in winter. Strong gray legs and long, somewhat thickly-based bill give an impression of solidity. Black and white wings diagnostic at all times.
Voice *Pee-wee-wee.*
Habitat Damp grasslands and pond shores; winters on lagoons, estuaries.
Range Breeds in central Rockies and northern prairies into Canada.
Movements Migrates to all coasts to winter and into South America.

Greater Yellowlegs
Tringa melanoleuca
12½–15in/32–38cm

Identification Mottled black
and white above to produce
a gray impression; white
below with some
streaking on neck and
breast. Long, thickish, slightly
upturned bill; long yellow legs.
In flight, shows uniform wing, white
rump and trailing legs. _See_ Lesser
Yellowlegs.
Voice Loud _keu-keu-keu_.
Habitat Breeds between boreal and
tundra zones – taiga; winters fresh marshes, lakes.
Range Breeds in band from southern Alaska to Newfoundland.
Movements Winters across southern US and along all three
coasts, southwards to South America.

Lesser Yellowlegs F.
Tringa flavipes
9½–11in/24–28cm

Identification Superficially similar to Greater Yellowlegs, but
much more lightly and more elegantly built. Gray above, white
below, but with longer neck, smaller head, pencil-thin straight bill.
Legs yellow and proportionately longer. Uniform wing and white
rump in flight.
Voice _Yoo-yoo._
Habitat Tundra and taiga marshes and bogs in summer; winters
fresh marshes.
Range More northerly than Greater Yellowlegs from Alaska and
Canadian arctic to Hudson's Bay.
Movements Winters, Gulf Coast and Florida southwards.

Stilt Sandpiper
Micropalama himantopus
8–8½in/20–22cm

Identification In summer, brown
above with heavily and
completely barred
underparts. Also chestnut
eye stripe and ear coverts. In winter,
is gray above and white below with
clear dark eyestripe. At all times,
long grayish legs and long, slightly
drooping bill are useful, giving the bird
a peculiar, if not unique, shape. White rump shows in flight.
Voice *Tu-tu.*
Habitat Tundra in summer; freshwater shores in winter.
Range Breeds on central Canadian tundra.
Movements Winters South America.

Short-billed Dowitcher
Limnodromus griseus
10–12in/26–30cm

Identification Very
similar to Long-billed
Dowitcher and to be distinguished
at all seasons with the greatest of care.
These are chunky, large-bodied
waders that have long, straight
bills and feed with a vigorous
probing motion. In summer they
are spangled chestnut and black above; chestnut with bars and
spots below. The length of bill is of little value in the field and
there is considerable overlap. In flight, both species show a narrow
white wing-bar on the secondaries and a white 'V' extending up
the rump. Both have green legs. The main differences are that the
present species has a white tail with narrow black bars, whereas
the Long-billed has a black tail with narrow white bars.
Additionally, the present species has black chestnut striped tertials
in summer and autumn, including juveniles.
Voice Melodic *tu-tu-tu.*
Habitat Boreal marshes; winters, estuaries.
Range Breeds coastal Alaska, central northern Canada.
Movements Winters all coasts southwards of California and South
Carolina.

Long-billed Dowitcher ꜰ
Limnodromus scolopaceus 10½−12½in/27−32cm

Identification A chunky, long-billed shorebird, very similar to Long-billed Dowitcher. For distinctions see that species. Generally darker, with a darker tail than that bird.
Voice Shrill *keek*.
Habitat Tundra bogs; winters found more often on fresh marshes than Short-billed.
Range Breeds western Alaska and adjacent north coast of Canada.
Movements Winters, coastal US from Washington to Florida.

Ruddy Turnstone
Arenaria interpres
8½−9½in/22−24cm

Identification Stocky wader, found only along shorelines, with short, stubby bill and stone-turning habits. In summer, has a 'harlequin' 'face' pattern in black and white with rich chestnut and black wings. In winter, smudgy 'face' pattern and grayish upperparts; legs, short and red. In flight, shows white 'braces' and wing-bar.
Voice Sharp *tuk-a-tuk*.
Habitat Rocky and muddy coasts; breeds on tundra islands.
Range Far northern Canada and archipelago and coastal Alaska.
Movements Winters on all coasts of US.

Purple Sandpiper
Calidris maritima 8–8½in/20–22cm

Identification A rocky coast shorebird that is easily overlooked in dull winter plumage. In summer is heavily spotted above and below with short orange legs and orange-based bill. In winter, foreparts more uniform gray with spotting below. At all times dumpy shape is important feature.

Voice Quiet *wut-wut*.

Habitat Tundra in summer; winters rocky coasts.

Range Breeds central Canadian tundra.

Movements Winters east coast as far south as Carolina.

Pectoral Sandpiper
Calidris melanotos 7–8½in/18–21cm

Identification Stocky shorebird marked by large, plump body with short, thin neck and small head and shortish orange-yellow legs. In all plumages, shape, plus uniformly streaked neck and breast ending abruptly to form clear-cut pectoral band, are best field marks.

Voice Far carrying *kreet*.

Habitat Summer tundra; passage and winter fresh marshes, pond margins.

Range Breeds northern coasts of Alaska and Canada.

Movements Mainly a migrant, especially on east coast. Winters South America.

Red Knot ⼲
Calidris canutus 9½–10½in/24–27cm

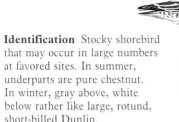

Identification Stocky shorebird
that may occur in large numbers
at favored sites. In summer,
underparts are pure chestnut.
In winter, gray above, white
below rather like large, rotund,
short-billed Dunlin.
Voice Dull *nut*.
Habitat Arctic tundra; winters on shorelines and estuaries.
Range Central Canadian archipelago.
Movements Winters coasts of California, Gulf Coast, Florida and
Atlantic.

Dunlin
Calidris alpina 6–7½in/16–19cm

Identification Stocky little shorebird marked by black belly in
summer. In winter, gray above, white below with streaking on
breast. In all plumages relatively long, slightly decurved bill is good
feature. Juvenile is warm buffy above and on breast, but is always
streaked.
Voice Nasal *tree*.
Habitat Breeds tundra; passage and winters coastal marshes,
shorelines, estuaries.
Range Alaskan and Canadian tundra east to Hudson's Bay.
Movements Winters all coasts.

Sanderling
Calidris alba 7½–8½in/19–22cm

Identification A neat little
shorebird, most often
seen in small flocks
running up and down
beaches following the
movements of the surf. In winter, pale gray plumage with black at
bend of wing is diagnostic. In summer, rich chestnut head, back
and breast are heavily spotted black. Shortish black bill.
Voice Rippling *kip-kip*.
Habitat Tundra; sandy beaches in winter.
Range Canadian archipelago.
Movements Winters along all coasts.

White-rumped Sandpiper
Calidris fuscicollis 6–7in/16–18cm

Identification Neat little shorebird with shortish black legs and
short, straight bill. Slimline accentuated by long wings projecting
beyond tail. Generally grayish, with streaking on breast extending
as 'arrowheads' along flanks, particularly in breeding plumage.
Juvenile has chestnut wash on back and crown. In flight shows
white rump.
Voice Shrill *jeet*.
Habitat Tundra; passage and winters marshes and estuaries.
Range Northern and archipelago coasts of Alaska and Canada.
Movements Moves mainly south and east to winter in South
America.

Baird's Sandpiper

Calidris bairdii

6½–7½in/17–19cm

Identification A short-legged,
short-billed sandpiper with long
wings accentuating slim,
elongated appearance. In all
plumages, warm, buffy wash over
scaly upperparts and streaked breast creates impression of a
'brown' rather than 'gray' bird.

Voice Harsh *kreep*.

Habitat Tundra; on passage on marshes and pond-edges.

Range Breeds northern Alaska and Canada, extending northwards
into the archipelago.

Movements Moves southwards through the Central Flyway to
South America.

Least Sandpiper

Calidris minutilla 5–5½in/13.5–14.5cm

Identification Tiny sandpiper with short, thin bill slightly
downcurved and yellow legs: the latter may be muddy and appear
dark. In summer and winter, breast-streaking forms a band; juvenile
has buffy breast with streaking at sides. Scaly upperparts with rich,
buffy feather margins; hint of pale inverted 'V' on back.

Voice High-pitched *kreep*.

Habitat Tundra; on passage and, in winter, marshes, pools,
lagoons.

Range In summer from Alaska across arctic Canada to Labrador.

Movements On passage throughout North America to winter
through southern states and along all coasts.

Semipalmated Sandpiper
Calidris pusilla 5½–6in/14–16cm

Identification Common, small shorebird with partially webbed feet that are virtually impossible to see in the field. Short, straight bill with thick base and blunt tip. Upperparts with feathers edged buff to create a regular, uniform pattern. This latter feature is important when comparing with easily confused Western Sandpiper.

Voice An abrupt *chirk*.

Habitat Tundra; on passage, marshes, pools, sheltered bays.

Range Breeds northern Alaska across Canada to Labrador.

Movements Passes through centre and east coast on way to South America to winter.

Western Sandpiper
Calidris mauri 6–6½in/15.5–17cm

Identification Of all the 'peep' (small sandpipers) this is the longest legged and longest billed, but it is still easy to confuse with Semipalmated Sandpiper. In summer, this bird has chestnut on crown, ear coverts and back and and is marked by extensive streaking on breast with 'arrow-like' markings on sides of neck and flanks. Juvenile has chestnut on scapulars and an irregular feather pattern on folded wings: compare with uniform scaly upperparts of Semipalmated. Also has less pronounced eyebrow.

Voice High-pitched *jeet*.

Habitat Breeds tundra; winters marshes, bays.

Range Breeds north and west coastal Alaska.

Movements Winters all coasts, often common on passage.

Wilson's Phalarope

Phalaropus tricolor 8½–10in/22–26cm

Identification Less inclined to swim
than other phalaropes. In summer,
female has bold chestnut 'S'
extending from the eye,
along the side of the neck
to trail over the back. Male is
similar, but duller and darker.
In winter, pale gray above,
white below with thin, needle-
like bill 1½ times length of head.
No black comma behind eye as in
other phalaropes.
Voice A croak.
Habitat Marshes.
Range Breeds over much of western North America extending
eastward through Great Lakes and increasing in eastern Canada.
Movements Winters in South America, moving southwards
mainly along west coast.

Red Phalarope Grey Phalarope

Phalaropus fulicarius 7½–8½in/19–21cm

Identification A swimming shorebird that spends the winter at
sea. In summer, rich chestnut underparts and white 'face' preclude
confusion. In winter, gray above, white below with dark comma
extending from eye. Bill, thick and yellow-based compared with
other phalaropes' needle-thin ones.
Voice High *twit*.
Habitat Tundra, on passage along coasts; winters at sea.
Range Tundra coasts of Alaska, Canada and archipelago.
Movements Mostly seen on passage wind blown to coasts.

Red-necked Phalarope
Phalaropus lobatus 6½–7½in/17–19cm

Identification Small, delicate phalarope. In summer, gray with white chin and red neck patch. In winter, gray with black comma behind eye. Shortish, needle-like bill. Juvenile much darker above.
Voice Quiet *tit*.
Habitat Tundra pool; winters at sea.
Range Alaskan and Canadian tundra.
Movements Migrates along coasts to winter at sea.

American Woodcock
Scolopax minor 6–11in/16–28cm

Identification A rotund, round-winged bird that is found in moist woodlands. Most often seen when flushed, or at dawn and dusk in spring when performing its nuptial flight. Chunky shape with rounded wings and long, straight, downward-pointing bill are best features. If seen in daylight, black bars on crown and streaked black back contrast with brown wings. Highly camouflaged.
Voice A repeated *peent*.
Habitat Damp woods.

Range Eastern half of US and adjacent Canada.
Movements Abandons northern half of US range.

Common Snipe
Gallinago gallinago
10−10½in/25−27cm

Identification Highly camouflaged
marshland bird heavily streaked in
brown, black and buff with bold,
double 'V' in cream on back. Long,
straight bill is probed vigorously
while feeding. When flushed, towers
with zig-zag flight into the air.
Nuptial flight consists of series of
aerial dives with stiff outertail
feathers vibrating to produce
a bleeting sound.
Voice Harsh *scarp.*
Habitat Wide variety of marshes.
Range Throughout Alaska and Canada, except northernmost
tundra, southwards through northern US.
Movements Winters in east, west and southern states.

Parasitic Jaeger
Stercorarius parasiticus
15−19in/38−48cm

Identification Dark, athletic
seabird that pursues other seabirds
to rob them of food. In summer,
adult has two extended tail feathers projecting
in flight, but these are often broken by the fall.
At all times this is a narrow-winged, angular jaeger
that is smaller than Pomarine and heavier than
Long-tailed. Pale phase birds have dark cap and pale
underparts with ill-defined dark breast band. Dark
phase birds are uniform brown. Both show white flashes in dark
wings.
Voice High-pitched *kee-ow* on breeding grounds.
Habitat Arctic tundra; passage and winter and sea.
Range Breeds Alaska, Northern Canada and in archipelago.
Movements Migrates along west coast, less numerous off east
coast, to winter at sea off South America.

Pomarine Jaeger
Stercorarius pomarinus
17–21in/43–53cm

Identification Summer adult has extended central tail feathers, blunt-tipped and twisted. In autumn, heavy build and, in pale phase birds, prominent breast band are best features. In all, plumages has more white in wing flashes than other jaegers.
Voice Silent at sea.
Habitat Tundra in summer; at sea in winter.
Range Breeds north coasts of Alaska, Canada and archipelago.
Movements Moves southward along west coast, rather scarce off east coast.

Long-tailed Jaeger
Stercorarius longicaudus
15–22in/38–56cm

Identification Smallest and most lightly built of the jaegers, more tern-like than others. Summer adult has long tail streamers. In fall, shows little, if any, white wing flash; but contrast between grayish upperparts and all-black flight feathers. Juvenile shows white wing flashes on under surface. At all times, size and build are best features.
Voice Silent at sea.
Habitat Summer, tundra; winter, sea.
Range Western and northern Alaska, northern Canada and archipelago; winters off South America.
Movements Scarcest of jaegers on passage, more regular west than east coast.

Great Skua
Stercorarius skua
22–24in/56–61cm

Identification Heavily-built, all-brown
jaeger with broad wings marked by bold,
white flash. Body has rufous wash and is heavily
streaked, creating a subtle contrast with darker, more uniformly
brown wings. South Polar Skua is rare, mainly in west, and is more
uniformly dark gray-brown.
Voice Nasal *skeer.*
Habitat Bare hills in summer; winters at sea.
Range Breeds in northern Europe.
Movements Regular offshore, east coast on passage.

Glaucous Gull
Larus hyperboreus
23–27in/58–69cm

Identification Large, pale
gray gull, with broadly white-
tipped flight feathers, that
lacks contrasting wing tip
pattern of most other pale
gulls. Adult has yellow
bill with red spot and
pink legs. Pale eye creates
a fierce expression. Juvenile is
spotted buffy, has pale, creamy wings and pink base to bill.
Voice Harsh *kyow.*
Habitat Breeds tundra; winters, coasts and some inland waters.
Range Breeds coastal Alaska, Canada and to Labrador.
Movements Winters ice-free coasts in east and west and among
Great Lakes.

Iceland Gull

Larus glaucoides 20–22½in/51–57cm

Identification Very similar to Glaucous Gull with white flight feathers and pale gray mantle. Slightly smaller, with rounded head and more gentle expression. Juvenile has all-black bill.
Voice Shrill *kyow*.
Habitat Breeds tundra coasts; winters coasts.
Range Breeds eastern Baffin Island.
Movements Winters, east coast from Newfoundland to Virginia.

Great Black-backed Gull

Larus marinus 25–27in/63–69cm

Identification Huge gull with equally huge, heavy bill. Adult is all-black across upperparts to wing tips, broken only by white terminal mirrors. Juvenile spotted brown and buff appearing paler and more contrasting than other juvenile large gulls. Bill yellow with red spot, legs pale pink.
Voice Hard *owk*.
Habitat Coasts.
Range Breeds eastern Canada southwards along adjacent US coasts.
Movements Resident, though some birds to move southwards as far as Florida.

Herring Gull
Larus argentatus
21½−23½in/54−60cm

Identification Gray-mantled, medium-sized gull with contrasting black wing tips marked by white mirrors. Bill, yellow with red spot, legs pink. Juvenile is mottled in shades of brown and, in flight, has pale inner primaries with dark terminal spots.
Voice Loud *kyow-kyow.*
Habitat Coasts.
Range Breeds over much of northern Canada. Alaska and extending southwards through the eastern US. Most abundant coastal gull in most areas.
Movements Winters along Pacific coasts of Canada and US, on Atlantic and Gulf coasts and inland on Great Lakes and southern and eastern US.

California Gull
Larus californicus
19½−21½in/50−54cm

Identification Like smaller, darker Herring Gull with less massive, more rounded head and yellow bill with black and red spots. Legs are greenish yellow. Gray mantle, black wing tips with white mirrors. Juvenile is dark with pinkish legs.
Voice Yelping *kyow.*
Habitat Breeds on inland marshes and lakes; winters, coast.
Range Breeds on prairies and plateaux in Rockies.
Movements Pacific Coast from southern British Columbia to Mexico.

Ring-billed Gull
Larus delawarensis 17–18½in/43–47cm

Identification Pale
gray gull with black wing
tips and white mirrors.
Bill, yellow with clear
black vertical bar; legs
yellow. In winter, spotted on crown and nape. From second winter,
eye is pale creating a fierce expression. Immature, brown with
grayish legs and dark eye, may be difficult to separate from Mew
Gull, but has larger bill and head and is more spotted.
Voice Loud *kyow*.
Habitat Marshes and lakes in summer; in winter also along coasts.
Range Breeds in prairies and plateaux of Rockies eastwards
through Great Lakes.
Movements Winters all coasts and inland especially in southern
and eastern states.

Mew Gull
Larus canus
15–17in/38–43cm

Identification Gray-
backed gull with black
wing tips and large white
mirrors. Gentle appearance,
with rounded head, smallish
yellow bill and yellow
legs. Immatures have
pink bills with black
tips and grayish legs. First winter birds can be confused with
similar aged Ring-billed, but head and bill shape distinct.
Voice High-pitched *kee-ar*.
Habitat tundra marshes in summer; coasts in winter.
Range Breeds Alaska and north-western Canada.
Movements Winters Pacific Coast.

Black-legged Kittiwake

Rissa tridactyla 15–17in/38–43cm

Identification Gray-backed gull
with long, narrow wings and
pure black wing tips.
Legs black and short,
bill yellow. In winter,
adult has dark smudge on nape.
Immature has black 'W' across wings
and black bar across nape. Abundant
at cliff breeding colonies.
Voice Repeated *kitti-waak.*
Habitat Cliffs in summer; at sea in
winter.
Range Breeds Alaska, Canadian archipelago, Newfoundland and
Gulf of St Lawrence.
Movements Disperses over northern Pacific and Atlantic, but
regularly seen along both coasts.

Laughing Gull

Larus atricilla 14½–16in/37–41cm

Identification A black-hooded gull with dark gray upperparts and
extensive black tips to wings. Bill is large, red and droopy; legs are
black. A narrow, white eye-ring is present in all plumages. In
winter, hood is lost and replaced by dark around eye and on hind
crown. Immatures have dusky breast.
Voice Low chuckles.
Habitat Coasts.
Range Atlantic Coast southward from Maine to Mexico.
Movements Northern breeders move southward.

Franklin's Gull
Larus pipixcan
13−14in/33−36cm

Identification Black-hooded, summer visitor to prairies. In summer, upperparts are slate-gray marked by white wing tips broken by line of black mirrors. Underwing, uniform silver. Red bill and legs; bold white eye-ring. In winter, has remnant hood, particularly noticeable on ear coverts; shows white eye-ring prominently. Immatures similar to winter adult, with white breast and brownish, mottled wing. Often hawks insects in air.
Voice High pitched chuckle.
Habitat Lakes and marshes.
Range Breeds prairies and upland grasslands.
Movements Migrates through interior and Gulf Coast; rare winter visitor there and California.

Bonaparte's Gull
Larus philadelphia
12−13in/30−33cm

Identification Smallest regular gull marked by black head in summer and black spot behind the eye in winter. In flight, shows bold white forewing, both above and below, with trailing wing edge of black primary tips. Small black bill, short red legs.
Voice Chattering.
Habitat Tundra and muskeg ponds and marshes.
Range In broad band from Alaska through Canada almost to the Great Lakes.
Movements Winters, Great Lakes and all coasts of US.

Sabine's Gull

Xema sabini 12½–13½in/32–34cm

Identification Adult in summer has black outer primaries, white inner primaries and secondaries, contrasting with warm gray wing coverts and forming a unique flight pattern. Slate-gray hood, bordered by narrow black line, and black bill with yellow tip, are best features at rest, though primaries show white mirrors that are never obvious in flight. Hood lost in winter though some dusky on head and partial border remains. Black legs. Tail neatly notched. Flashes black and white in flight.
Voice Tern like.
Habitat Tundra coasts; winters at sea.
Range Western and northern coasts of Alaska, north and archipelago coasts of Canada.
Movements Reasonably common off Pacific Coast. Northern and eastern birds head eastwards over Atlantic to coasts of south-western Europe.

Least Tern

Sterna albifrons 9–10in/23–26cm

Identification Smallest tern marked by gray upperparts, white below with black cap and peaked white forehead. Bill and feet yellow, the former tipped black. Long narrow wings, frequently hovers, dives for food.
Voice High *ki-tik*.
Habitat Shorelines, beaches, sand bars.
Range Breeds all US coastlines and along Mississippi River system.
Movements Moves south in winter.

Arctic Tern
Sterna paradisaea
12–15in/30–39cm

Identification Summer adult
is pale gray above and below
with black cap and white
cheeks. Bill is blood-red, legs
short and red. Tail deeply
forked. First winter has
white trailing edge
to inner wing.
To be distinguished
with care from Common Tern.
Voice *Key-rrr.*
Habitat Tundra marshes; winters at sea.
Range Breeds across whole of northern Canada and Alaska and, in
the east, south to Nova Scotia.
Movements Long distance migrant to southern oceans.

Common Tern
Sterna hirundo
12–14in/30–36cm

Identification Pale gray
above, paler below with
black cap, but no
contrasting white
cheek patch. Bill
orange-red with black
tip (sometimes absent); legs orange-
red. First winter, has dark trailing edge to wing
contrasting with paler mid-wing panel. *See* Arctic Tern.
Voice High *kirri-kirri.*
Habitat Marshes, pools, lagoons, beaches.
Range Mainly across southern Canada eastwards of Rockies, but
southwards across the US border.
Movements Winters on coasts of South America.

Roseate Tern Same

Sterna dougallii
12½–15½in/32–40cm

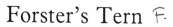

Identification Smaller than
Common and Arctic Terns, but
with longer tail streamers.
Summer adult very pale
gray above with white
underparts washed
with warm pinkish flush.
Always whiter than other similar
sized terns. Bill, black, variable red
base; legs, red.
Voice Quiet *kee-aa*.
Habitat Beaches, islands, coasts;
winters at sea.
Range Scarce breeder east coast US.
Movements Winters to the south.

Forster's Tern F.

Sterna forsteri 13½–15in/34–38cm

Identification Like Common Tern, gray above and white below.
Red bill with black tip; longer red legs. Tail, long and forked. In
flight, shows white primaries and white edges to tail. In winter,
black cap becomes bold black mark behind eye, bill all black.
Voice *Ky-aar*.
Habitat Marshes, scarce on coasts.
Range Breeds on prairies and plateaux among Rockies; also on
Gulf Coast marshes and locally on Atlantic Coast.
Movements Winters, Gulf Coast, Florida, Atlantic Coast as far
north as the Carolinas.

Sandwich Tern ☞.

Sterna sandvicensis 15–17in/38–43cm

Identification Large, pale tern with long, pointed black bill, tipped yellow. Adult in summer is pale gray, as pale as Roseate and Gull-billed, with ragged black crest. Legs are black, tail forked. Breeds in dense colonies. In winter, black confined to rear crest.
Voice Harsh *kee-rick*.
Habitat Shorelines, coastal marshes, sand bars.
Range Breeds, Atlantic and Gulf coasts of US.
Movements Winters, Gulf Coast and Florida.

Gull-billed Tern ☞.

Gelochelidon nilotica 14–15in/35–39cm

Identification Large, pale gray tern with thick, bull-necked appearance and large, deep black bill. As pale as Sandwich Tern, but distinctive heavy shape. Legs black and long for a tern. Hawks insects over dry land and wetlands.
Voice Harsh *ka-wak*.
Habitat Coastal marshes.
Range Breeds, Atlantic and Gulf Coasts of US.
Movements Winters, Florida and Gulf Coast.

Royal Tern F.

Sterna maxima 17½–20in/45–51cm

Identification Similar to Elegant Tern, but with thicker, orange-red bill. In winter, black crest starts behind (not at) black eye. Legs, black.
Voice High pitched *chirrip*.
Habitat Coasts.
Range Breeds on Gulf and Atlantic coasts.
Movements Winters, southern California, Gulf and Atlantic coasts and Florida.

Caspian Tern F.

Sterna caspia 19–22in/48–56cm

Identification Huge gray tern with massive coral red bill. Black cap in summer, mottled in winter. Legs long and black.
Voice Hard *kraa.*
Habitat Coasts, lakes, rivers.
Range Locally along all coasts and inland as far north as tundra; very disjointed.
Movements Winters, Gulf Coast, Florida and adjacent Atlantic Coast.

Black Tern
Chlidonias niger
9–10in/23–26cm

Black Tern

Identification Adult in summer is black with slate-gray wings and white undertail. In winter, is white below, slate-gray above with black cap and dark smudge at side of breast. Hawks insects over water.
Voice High-pitched *kik*.
Habitat Marshes, lakes.
Range Breeds right across temperate Canada and throughout northern and western states.
Movements Regular migrant to South America.

Black Skimmer
Rynchops niger
16½–18in/42–46cm

Identification Black above, white below, with black crown extending to eye; white forehead. Huge, mis-shapen red and black bill. Skims over water.
Voice Deep *oow*.
Habitat Coastal bays and marshes.
Range Breeds, Atlantic and Gulf coasts.
Movements Leaves northern parts of Atlantic Coast in winter.

Razorbill

Razorbill

Alca torda 15–17in/39–43cm

Identification Chunky seabird, similar to Common Murre, but with deep black bill marked by white vertical line. Black above extends to breast in summer, but only to sides of head in winter. Flies with fast wing beats.
Voice Grunts.
Habitat Broken cliffs in summer; offshore in winter.
Range Breeds on coasts of Labrador southward to Gulf of St Lawrence.
Movements Winters near breeding grounds and as far south as Maryland.

Common Murre

Guillemot

Uria aalge 15½–17i/40–44cm.

Identification Chunky, short-winged seabird with blackish upperparts washed with dark brown. Bill is pointed. In summer, dark upperparts extend to breast; in winter, only to sides of head. A varying proportion of Atlantic birds have a bridle of white eye-ring and line across cheek.
Voice Growls.
Habitat High-cliffs, winters at sea.
Range Breeds from Labrador to Gulf of St Lawrence in east; and from western Alaska to coast of California in west.
Movements Winters at sea near breeding colonies.

Thick-billed Murre
Uria lomvia 16–18in/41–46cm

Identification Very similar to Common
murre, but blacker with thicker bill and
pale line along base of upper mandible.
In winter, shows darker face than
Common Murre.
Voice Growls.
Habitat Cliffs; winters at sea.
Range Overlaps with, but
breeds farther north than
Common Murre. Abundant among
Canadian archipelago, in Alaska and
locally in Labrador.
Movements Seldom progresses much farther south than breeding
grounds, though may be commonest Murre off east coast of US.

Dovekie Little Auk
Alle alle 8–8½in/20–22cm

Identification Only tiny auk of Atlantic Coast. Dumpy shape,
narrow rounded wings, and tiny stubby bill added to size preclude
confusion. Neck and breast, black in summer, white in winter.
Breeds in enormous colonies in far north.
Voice Silent at sea.
Habitat Tundra screes; winters at sea.
Range Breeds only eastern coasts of Greenland.
Movements Winters over Atlantic and may be seen off east coasts,
particularly after storms.

Black Guillemot

Cepphus grylle 13–14in/33–35cm

Identification All-black auk marked by
white ovals on wings. In winter, head,
neck and underparts are white,
wings black with white
ovals, upperparts barred
dark gray. In flight, shows
white underwings in all
plumages and white on
inner wing above. *See*
Pigeon Guillemot.
Voice Various whistles.
Habitat Broken bases of cliffs;
winters inshore.
Range Breeds from Canadian archipelago eastwards
to St Lawrence and Nova Scotia. Also in northern Alaska.
Movements Winters near breeding colonies.

Atlantic Puffin

Fratercula arctica 11½–12in/29–31cm

Identification Only Atlantic puffin. Upperparts, black extending
to crown and breast, with silvery-white face; underparts, white.
Large red, yellow and black bill in
summer. Legs, red. In winter,
'face' becomes gray and bill
becomes less clearly colored.
Juvenile has narrower,
pointed bill.
Voice deep *arr-arr*.
Habitat Cliff tops and cliff
slides in summer; in winter at
sea.
Range Breeds from Labrador
to Gulf of St Lawrence.
Movements Winters near
breeding colonies and at sea. Seldom
seen south of New England.

Rock Dove
Columba livia 11½–12½in/29–32cm

Identification The town
pigeon with a wide variety of plumages.
Pure wild birds are gray with two black wing bars and white rump.
Voice *Ooo-roo-coo*, repeated.
Habitat Cliffs, cities.
Range Whole of temperate North America.
Movements Resident.

White-winged Dove
Zenaida asiatica 10½–11½in/27–29cm

Identification Dark, olive-green dove with bold white wing
patches, obvious both at rest and in flight. White tipped tail shows
well.
Voice *Hooo-hooo-hoo-hooo.*
Habitat Dry woods, orchards, semi-desert.
Range Mexican border, locally abundant.
Movements Winters, Mexico and Gulf Coast to Florida.

Mourning Dove
Zenaida macroura
11½–12in/29–31cm

Identification Brown upperparts
spotted black; rich pinkish on breast.
In flight, appears uniformly dark, but
long pointed tail has brown white
margins.
Voice *Oooh-oo-oo-oo.*
Habitat Farms, towns, cities.
Range Most widespread pigeon. Breeds throughout US and
southern Canada.
Movements Northern birds move southwards to winter.

Scaly-breasted Ground Dove ♀
Columbina passerina 6–7in/16–18cm

Identification Gray-brown above with black spots on folded
wings. Male has gray crown and pinkish breast, heavily scaled.
Female is grayer. In flight, shows rusty outer wing. *See* Inca Dove.
Voice *Hoo-ah* rising.
Habitat Brush country and open ground.
Range Mexican border country and across Gulf Coast states to
Florida.
Movements Resident.

Inca Dove

Columbina inca 7½–8½in/19–22cm

Identification Similar to Scaly-breasted Ground Dove, but heavily marked with scaly crescents above and below. Shows chestnut in wing, particularly in flight, but also has long, rounded tail with black and white margins.
Voice *Coo-coo.*
Habitat Dry semi-desert, often near buildings.
Range Mexican border country.
Movements Resident.

Yellow-billed Cuckoo

Coccyzus americanus
10½–11½in/27–29cm

Identification Slim, long-tailed bird; brown above and white below. Stout, pointed bill has yellow lower mandible, but separated from similar Black-billed Cuckoo by rust in wings, and boldly barred black and white undertail.
Voice Sharp *kuk-kuk-kuk.*
Habitat Woodland, groves.
Range Throughout US, but scarce or absent California and northwest states. Barely penetrates southernmost Canada.
Movements Summer visitor.

Black-billed Cuckoo
Coccyzus erythrophthalmus
10½−11½in/27−29cm

Identification Similar shape, size
and coloration as Yellow-billed
Cuckoo. Separated by having no
rust in wing and only tips of tail
feathers marked black and white.
Voice *Co-co-co.*
Habitat Streamside woods.
Range Northern, eastern and
central US, together with
southern Canada.
Movements Summer visitor.

Greater Roadrunner
Geococcyz californianus 22−23in/56−59cm

Identification Well known,
ground-dwelling bird with
heavily spotted
upperparts, bold crest,
large black bill and extremely
long, black tail. A great
runner.
Voice Pigeon-like
cooing.
Habitat Mesquite
and semi-desert.
Range South-western US.
Movements Resident.

Screech Owl

Otus asio 8½–9in/21–23cm

Identification Variably colored small
owl that is often divided into two distinct
species. Yellow eyes, prominent ear tufts,
bold white spots across folded wing and
black-edged, facial disc are all good
features.
Voice Wavering whistles and a trill.
Habitat Woods, parks, suburbs.
Range Throughout US northwards along coast of British
Columbia to Alaska.
Movements Resident.

Great Horned Owl

Bubo virginianus 22–23in/53–58cm

Identification Huge,
powerful owl, with large
rounded wings. Upperparts
are mottled and barred brown;
underparts streaked and closely
barred. Prominent ear tufts,
facial disc and yellow eyes.
Voice Deep *hooo-hoo-hoo*.
Habitat Forests, mountains,
suburbs, parks.
Range Throughout North America save extreme northern tundra.
Movements Resident.

Long-eared Owl
Asio otus
13½–14½in/34–37cm

Identification Medium-sized owl with heavy streaking above and below and prominent ear tufts, facial disc and yellow-orange eyes. Totally nocturnal. Appears tall and slim when discovered perched.
Voice A low *hoo*.
Habitat Forests and woods.
Range Breeds throughout North America south of the tree line, though absent from southern states.
Movements Many boreal-zone birds migrate south. Winters, throughout US, including areas of south where it does not breed.

Short-eared Owl
Asio flammeus 14–15in/36–39cm

Identification Long-winged, diurnal owl that mostly frequents rough ground and marshes. Buffy and heavily streaked above and below, with clear-cut facial disc and yellow eyes. Glides and hovers in search of prey.
Voice Barking in breeding season.
Habitat Marshes, rough ground, tundra.
Range Breeds throughout Canada and the northern half of the US.
Movements Migrates from Canada to winter over most of the US.

Barn Owl
Tyto alba 13–14in/33–36cm

Identification Ghost-like, white-breasted owl with cinnamon upperparts that often hunts late in the day or in the early morning. Breast color varies from white to pale cinnamon.
Voice Hissing and snoring calls.
Habitation Farmland, suburbs, woodland, parks.
Range Breeds across US, though absent from central northern states.
Movements Largely resident.

Snowy Owl
Nyctea scandiaca
21–26in/51–54cm

Identification Large white owl of tundra. Smaller male is white with variable black spotting on wings and flanks. Female is more heavily spotted and barred all over. Rounded head appears small.
Voice Deep hooting.
Habitat Tundra.
Range Northernmost Alaska and Canada, including archipelago.
Movements Irregular in irruptive movements southward across Canada to northern states.

Barred Owl

Strix varia 20–21½in/51–54cm

Identification Medium-sized owl,
heavily barred above and streaked
below. Black bordered facial disc
with ringed face and dark eyes.
Voice *Oo-oo-ooo-oooo.*
Habitat Conifer and other dense
woodlands.
Range Breeds across eastern US and Canada
extending north and west to British Columbia;
colonising westwards.
Movements Resident.

Great Gray Owl

Strix nebulosa
25½–27½in/65–70cm

Identification Large gray owl,
spotted, barred and streaked
black. Huge head with facial
disc prominently ringed.
Small, yellow eyes. Hunts
dawn and dusk.
Voice Deep *who* repeated.
Habitat Boreal and mountain
conifer forests.
Range Boreal forests of Canada eastward to Great Lakes,
southward in Rockies to northern California.
Movements Mainly resident, but some birds do wander a little
southward.

Hawk Owl
Surnia ulula
15−16½in/39−42cm

Identification Long-tailed owl of northern forests that is often seen perched openly on a tree top in daylight. Dark gray, heavily spotted white above; heavily barred black below. White facial disc with yellow eyes, boldly bordered black. Long barred tail.
Voice Falcon-like *ki-ki-ki*.
Habitat Conifer forests.
Range Boreal Canada and Alaska from coast to coast.
Movements Resident.

Burrowing Owl
Athene cunicularia
9−10in/23−25cm

Identification Small, ground-dwelling owl with remarkably long legs. Upperparts brown, spotted white; underparts white, neatly barred brown. Head seems small and rounded with prominent white eyebrows and black chin patch. Often perches openly during day.
Voice Quick *coo-cooo*.
Habitat Dry open grassland.
Range Breeds over western half of US northwards just into Canada.
Movements Migrates southward; winters along Mexican border.

Boreal Owl
Aegolius funereus
9–10in/23–25cm

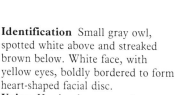

Identification Small gray owl,
spotted white above and streaked
brown below. White face, with
yellow eyes, boldly bordered to form
heart-shaped facial disc.
Voice *Hoo-hoo-hoo* repeated.
Habitat Conifer forests.
Range Boreal Canada to Alaska, also in several areas of Rockies.
Movements Resident.

Northern Saw-whet Owl
Aegolius acadicus 7½–8½in/19–21cm

Identification Small owl with brown upperparts liberally spotted
white; underparts white, boldly streaked rust. Facial disc is radially
streaked rufous and brown.
Voice Repeated single whistle.
Habitat Dense conifer and mixed forests.
Range Most of US and southern Canada extending northwards to
Alaska along Pacific coast. Absent central and southern states.
Movements Some movement to areas of center and south where it
does not breed.

Chuck-will's-widow
Caprimulgus carolinensis
11½–12in/29–31cm

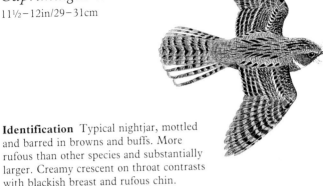

Identification Typical nightjar, mottled
and barred in browns and buffs. More
rufous than other species and substantially
larger. Creamy crescent on throat contrasts
with blackish breast and rufous chin.
Voice *Chuck-will's-widow.*
Habitat Woods and groves.
Range South-eastern quarter of US.
Movements Summer visitor, but resident Florida.

Whip-poor-will
Caprimulgus vociferus
9½–10in/24–26cm

Identification Grayish nightjar, considerably smaller than Chuck-
will's-widow. Black chin and white throat-crescent more prominent
in male, which has white tail corners in flight.
Voice *Whip-poor-will.*
Habitat Conifer and mixed woods.
Range Breeds most of eastern and south-western US.
Movements Migrates south, but winters in Florida and along
Gulf Coast.

Poor-will
Phalaenoptilus nuttallii
7½–8½in/19–21cm

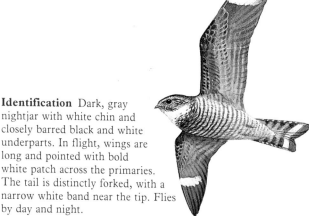

Identification Small nightjar
mottled in shades of gray and
brown, with white-tipped tail and
rounded wings. White throat-crescent
contrasts with dark chin and black
breast.
Voice *Poor-will.*
Habitat Dry open country.
Range Western half of US.
Movements Summer visitor, resident along Mexican border.

Common Nighthawk
Chordeiles minor 9–10in/23–25cm

Identification Dark, gray
nightjar with white chin and
closely barred black and white
underparts. In flight, wings are
long and pointed with bold
white patch across the primaries.
The tail is distinctly forked, with a
narrow white band near the tip. Flies
by day and night.
Voice Nasal *peent.*
Habitat Grasslands, woods, towns.
Range Virtually whole of sub-tundra North America.
Movements Summer visitor.

Lesser Nighthawk
Chordeiles acutipennis
8½−9in/21−23cm

Identification Similar to Common
Nighthawk, but paler and with less
clear-cut barring. Best distinctions
are more rounded wings, with
white primary patch nearer
wing tip; and notched (not
forked) tail with broad white
band and several smaller bands.
Voice Rapid trilling.
Habitat Dry scrub, semi-desert.
Range Mexican border states.
Movements Summer visitor.

Chimney Swift
Chaetura pelagica 4½−5in/12−13cm

Identification Dark brown
above and below, with paler
gray, buffy throat and upper
breast. Tail short and cut
abruptly square. Only swift
in the east and could be
confused only with
Vaux's Swift.
Voice Loud chatter.
Habitat Breeds in chimneys, trees.
Range US and southern Canada east of Rockies.
Movements Summer visitor.

White-throated Swift
Aeronautes saxatalis 6–6½in/16–17cm

Identification Large swift marked by bold black and white pattern above and below. Only swift with white on underparts. Tail distinctly forked.
Voice Shrill chattering.
Habitat Cliffs and canyons.
Range Mountains of the western US.
Movements Migrates, but resident in Mexican border states.

Ruby-throated Hummingbird
Archilochus colubris 4in/10cm

Identification Male is green above, white below, with metallic ruby-colored throat patch. The latter changes to black in some lights. Female lacks ruby-throat and is white on underparts. This is virtually the only hummingbird in the east, but beware Black-chinned Hummingbird where ranges meet. Females virtually inseparable.
Voice Squeaky *chip*.
Habitat Woodland edges, gardens.
Range Eastern half of US northwards across southern Canada.
Movements Summer visitor.

Broad-tailed Hummingbird
Selasphorus platycerus 4in/10cm

Identification Green above,
with metallic, ruby-colored throat
in male. Thus very similar to Ruby-
throated which it replaces in the west.
One of best features is that wing beats
produce a loud whistle. Female has white
throat and pale, rufous wash on flanks.
Voice Hard *chip*.
Habitat Mountain thickets, glades.
Range Rocky Mountains and foothills.
Movements Summer visitor.

Black-chinned Hummingbird
Archilochus alexandri 4in/10cm

Identification Male has
violet throat, becoming black
on chin, though in most lights the
'bib' looks totally black.
Female very similar to female
Ruby-throated.
Voice Quiet *tu*.
Habitat Dry scrub, open woods, suburbs.
Range Western and south-western US.
Movements Summer visitor; some winter in south-eastern states.

Belted Kingfisher
Ceryle alcyon 12½–13½in/32–34cm

Identification The only North American kingfisher. Male has blue-gray upperparts, crown and crest, and breast band. Breast and collar are white. Female differs in having a rich-chestnut breast band. The long bill is gray. This is a great hovering bird that dives to catch fish. Ringed Kingfisher of south-western Texas has underparts chestnut.
Voice Loud rattle.
Habitat Ponds, rivers, lakes, creeks.
Range Breeds throughout sub-tundra North America except south western US.
Movements Northern and central birds are migratory.

Northern Flicker
Colaptes auratus 12–13in/30–33cm

Identification North American flickers were, until recently, regarded as three separate species. Yellow-shafted, Red-shafted and Gilded. All are brown on back and wings spotted with black; white below, similarly spotted black with a black breast-crescent and white rump. Western birds have a red malar stripe; eastern birds a black one. In flight, the underwing is rufous (Red-shafted) or yellow. These are expert climbers that are frequently also seen on the ground.
Voice *Wik-wik-wik.*
Habitatio Woods, suburbs, but also remote areas.
Range From tundra southwards throughout North America, but absent central Texas.
Movements Most Canadian birds move southwards.

Pileated Woodpecker
Dryocopus pileatus 15½–17in/40–43cm

Identification Large, black woodpecker
with white facial lines and red crest. Male
also has red malar stripe. In flight,
underwing has white linings. Confusable
only with the presumed extinct Ivory-billed
Woodpecker which has white 'V' on back
and white secondaries forming a white
'lower back' when perched. In flight,
Ivory-bill has broad white trailing edge
to wings, both above and below.
Voice *Wucka-wucka-wucka.*
Habitat Forests and parks.
Range Breeds through most eastern states and westwards across
southern and central Canada. Also southwards through Pacific
states.
Movements Resident.

Red-bellied Woodpecker
Centurus carolinus 9½–10in/24–26cm

Identification Clearly-barred, black and white
upperparts create 'ladder-back'. Underparts, buffy
with red wash on belly. Male has whole crown red,
female only hind-crown. *See* Golden-fronted and
Gila Woodpeckers.
Voice *Churr.*
Habitat Open woods, suburbs.
Range Breeds through eastern US.
Movements Leaves northern states in winter.

Golden-fronted Woodpecker

Centurus aurifrons 9½–10in/24–26cm

Identification Similar to Red-bellied Woodpecker with black and white 'ladder-back'. Male has top of crown red, with golden nape and base of bill. Female lacks red on crown. Tail black, not barred.
Voice *Churr.*
Habitat Woods, groves.
Range Central Texas.
Movements Resident.

Ladder-backed Woodpecker

Picoides scalaris 6½–7½in/17–19cm

Identification Typical black and white woodpecker with black and white barred upperparts producing 'ladder-back'. Underparts buffy, spotted black. Male has red crown and distinctive black line across side of head enclosing the 'cheeks'. Female has similar face pattern and black crown.
Voice Sharp *pic.*
Habitat Dry semi-desert, towns.
Range States bordering Mexico.
Movements Resident.

Red-cockaded Woodpecker

Picoides borealis 8½–9in/21–23cm

Identification Similar to Ladder-backed Woodpecker, with similar black and white barring on upperparts. Underparts are white, not buffy, and black 'cheek' pattern is more open, creating a whiter head. Red confined to tiny dash at rear of ear coverts.
Voice Rasping *srip*.
Habitat Pine woods.
Range South-eastern states, declining.
Movements Resident.

Red-headed Woodpecker

Melanerpes erythrocephalus 9–10in/23–25cm

Identification Boldly black, white and red woodpecker. Adult has whole head red, upperparts black, with white rump and white secondaries.
Voice *Querk*.
Habitat Woods, parks, gardens.
Range US and southern Canada east of the Rockies.
Movements Northern and western birds are migrants.

Lewis' Woodpecker
Melanerpes lewis 10–11in/26–28cm

Identification Very dark, metallic-green
woodpecker with dark-red face, grayish-
pink belly and pale-gray collar, that is
particularly obvious in flight. Often
catches insects in air; gregarious
in winter.
Voice Mostly silent.
Habitat Open woods.
Range Throughout western states northward into British
Columbia.
Movements Northern birds migrate southwards.

Yellow-bellied Sapsucker
Sphyrapicus varius 8½in/21–22cm

Identification Highly variable bird; but
with black and white 'ladder-back', white wing
coverts and yellowish belly. Head and breast
color varies from black, white and red stripes to
uniformly red (in the now conspecific Red-breasted
Sapsucker). Excavates series of holes in trees to feed on
sap and insects attracted by it.
Voice Mostly silent.
Habitat Deciduous and conifer forests.
Range Most of North America except open plains.
Movements Whole population migrates south to winter in
southern states and Mexico.

Hairy Woodpecker
Picoides villosus 9–10in/23–24cm

Identification Medium-sized, pied woodpecker marked by white back and white barring on black wings. Black and white face pattern with red on rear crown of male.
See Downy Woodpecker.
Voice *Peek.*
Habitat Dense forests.
Range Most sub-tundra areas of North America.
Movements Resident.

Downy Woodpecker
Picoides pubescens 6–6½in/16–17cm

Identification Similarly marked, but much smaller version of Hairy Woodpecker with white back, barred wings and red spot on hind crown of male. Tiny bill is diagnostic.
Voice *Pik.*
Habitat Woods, parks, gardens.
Range Virtually whole of sub-tundra North America.
Movements Resident.

Black-backed Three-toed Woodpecker

Picoides arcticus
9–9½in/23–24cm

Identification Black above, white below, heavily barred black. Face pattern consists of finest of white lines behind eye and bold black zig-zag line across white cheek and neck. Male has golden crown, lacking in female.
Voice Hard *kip*.
Habitat Conifer forests.
Range Boreal Canada southwards through Rockies.
Movements Resident.

Northern Three-toed Woodpecker

Picoides tridactylus 8½in/21–22cm

Identification Similar to Black-backed Three-toed, but has white and black 'ladder-back' (sometimes pure white) and widening white stripe extending behind eye.
Voice *Pik*.
Habitat Conifer forests.
Range Boreal Canada southwards through Rockies.
Movements Resident.

Scissor-tailed Flycatcher f
Tyrannus forficatus
12½–13½in/32–34cm

Identification Adult, marked by very
long outer tail feathers creating
extremely deep forked tail. Head
and back dove gray; wings,
black with feathers broadly
edged white. Underparts,
rich pink, extending to
underwing linings.
Juvenile lacks extreme
tail length and pink on
underside; wing linings
show subdued pink.
Voice *Ka-leep.*
Habitat Farms, scrub, open country.
Range Southern western states, Texas and beyond.
Movements Summer visitor, some winter southernmost Florida.

Vermilion Flycatcher
Pyrocephalus rubinus 5½–6in/14–15cm

Identification Adult male
unmistakable with vividly red crown
and underparts. Female is buff-brown
above with dark ear coverts, streaked
breast and a warm, orange-red wash on
the belly. Immature male has red belly
and a few red feathers on throat and crown.
Immature female has yellow wash on belly.
Voice A pleasant *pit-a-see* repeated.
Habitat Aquatic woods and tangles.
Range Mexican border states.
Movements Northernmost birds move to Mexican border.

Eastern Kingbird
Tyrannus tyrannus
8½in/21–22cm

Identification Black
crown, dark gray back and
wings, with black tail, broadly tipped white.
Underparts are dusky white, with subtle gray
breast band. Generally perches openly.
Voice *Zeet* repeated.
Habitat Woodland edges, farms, usually near water.
Range Breeds over most of sub-tundra North America, but absent
from west and south-west.
Movements Summer visitor.

Western Kingbird
Tyrannus verticalis 8½in/21–22cm

Identification Gray head and breast,
yellow belly, olive-gray back combine
with black wings and tail, the latter
with white outer feathers. This is
the widespread tyrant flycatcher
of the west and forms a basis
from which other 'yellow'
flycatchers should be separated
with care. Perches openly,
upright, with large bill and
head prominent. Often
appears nervous.
Voice *Whit.*
Habitat Open country with scrub and fences.
Range Common over western US northward into adjacent
Canada.
Movements Summer visitor, migrant through eastern US.

Cassin's Kingbird
Tyrannus vociferans 8½–9in/22–23cm

Identification Very similar to Western
Kingbird, but buffy tips to tail and lack
of white margins are good features. Gray
head marked by whiter chin and pale
margins to wing feathers are further
distinction. Separate with care.
Voice *Chi-hew.*
Habitat Usually denser thickets in dry country than Western
Kingbird.
Range From coastal California through adjacent western states
northwards to Wyoming.
Movements Summer visitor.

Gray Kingbird F.
Tyrannus dominicensis 8½–9in/21–23cm

Identification Separated from Eastern Kingbird by larger size,
heavier bill and lack of black crown and back. Crown and back,
gray with darker area on lores and ear coverts. Underparts whitish,
wings with large gray margins; tail long and black.

Voice *Pe-cherree.*
Habitat Mangroves and scrub.
Range Common among Florida Keys, less so along adjacent
mainland coasts.
Movements Summer visitor.

Great Crested Flycatcher ⌗
Myiarchus crinitus 8½in/21–22cm

Identification Brown above
with distinct crest, pale margins to
wing coverts forming bold, white,
double wing-bar. Rusty margins to
flight feathers of wing and tail.
Easily confused with other
flycatchers, but gray throat, finely
streaked white, is darker than
similar species and tail is more rusty.
Voice Hard *wheep*.
Habitat Deciduous woods.
Range Eastern US northwards into adjacent Canada.
Movements Summer visitor; a few winter southern Florida.

Ash-throated Flycatcher
Myiarchus cinerascens 8½in/21–22cm

Identification Brown upperparts
with rust in tail and wing like
Great Crested. Pale gray throat
and pale yellow underparts
are best distinctions. Bill
thinner, generally paler
than other flycatchers.
Voice Short *ka-wheer*.
Habitat Western woods, scrub, semi-desert.
Range Breeds west of a line drawn from western Texas to Oregon.
Movements Summer visitor, a few winter extreme south-west US.

Eastern Phoebe

Sayornis phoebe 6½–7in/17–18cm

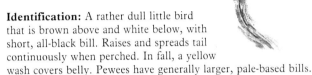

Identification: A rather dull little bird
that is brown above and white below, with
short, all-black bill. Raises and spreads tail
continuously when perched. In fall, a yellow
wash covers belly. Pewees have generally larger, pale-based bills.
Voice *Fee-be.*
Habitat Farms, suburbs.
Range Breeds over most of eastern US extending northwards
through Canadian prairies and beyond.
Movements Most birds are summer visitors, but winter along
Atlantic and Gulf coasts and over much of south-eastern US.

Black Phoebe

Sayornis nigricans 6–6½in/16–17cm

Identification Boldly black
and white bird with chunky
body and longish tail, which
is pumped up and down.
Black upperparts, head and
breast; white belly and outer
tail feathers. Juvenile is
browner above with rusty
margins to wing coverts.
Voice *Pee-wee.*
Habitat Stream and lake margins; parks in winter.
Range California and south-western US.
Movements Resident over most of range.

Say's Phoebe
Sayornis saya 7–7½in/18–19cm

Identification Buffy brown above, with
black tail and rusty belly and undertail coverts.
Though rather nondescript, the black tail is
wagged and spread like other phoebes.
Voice *Pee-ee.*
Habitat Dry rocky areas, farmsteads.
Range Whole of western North America from Alaska to western
Texas and into the prairies.
Movements Summer visitor, though some birds winter in south-
western US.

Yellow-billed Flycatcher
Empidonax flaviventris 5–5½in/13–14cm

Identification One of highly
confusing group of mainly
olive-colored flycatchers
marked by bold eye-ring and
pale, double wing-bar. Identification
often rests on minor plumage features.
This species has yellow throat,
extensive olive breast, tiny bill
with pale lower mandible.
Voice *Per-wee.*
Habitat Northern conifer forests.
Range Boreal Canada and north-eastern US.
Movements Summer visitor; scarce on migration.

Acadian Flycatcher

Empidonax virescens 5½–6in/14–15cm

Identification Very similar to Yellow-bellied Flycatcher. Pale eye-ring; bold, double wing-bar; lower mandible pale yellow; breast olive, separated from yellow belly by white on lower breast. Throat grayish.

Voice *Weez.*
Habitat Dense forests.
Range Only Empidonax flycatcher that breeds in eastern lowlands of US.
Movements Summer visitor.

Alder Flycatcher

Empidonax alnorum 5½–6in/14–15cm

Identification Darkish flycatcher with medium-strength eye-ring and long, black tail. Very similar to Willow Flycatcher with which previously regarded as conspecific; rather greener above and eye-ring much more obvious.
Voice *Fee-bew.*
Habitat Boggy woods of birch and alder in conifer zone.
Range Boreal Alaska and Canada to north-eastern US.
Movements Summer visitor.

Willow Flycatcher
Empidonax traillii 5½–6in/14–15cm

Identification Dark flycatcher,
even darker than closely related
Alder Flycatcher, from which
it should be separated only with
the greatest of care. Lack of eye-ring
is best field mark.
Voice *Fitz-beu.*
Habitat Meadows, streamsides, thickets.
Range Right across US, but absent from southern states.
Movements Summer visitor.

Least Flycatcher
Empidonax minimus
4½–5in/12–13cm

Identification Small flycatcher
with large-headed appearance, bold eye-ring and
dark olive, or olive-brown upperparts. White throat
and gray breast are good features; bill appears small
with pale base to lower mandible.
Voice *Che-bek.*
Habitat Open woodland, farmland, orchards.
Range From boreal zone southwards into the northern US.
Movements Summer visitor.

Dusky Flycatcher
Empidonax oberholseri
5½–6in/14–15cm

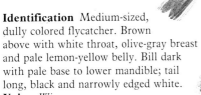

Identification Medium-sized,
dully colored flycatcher. Brown
above with white throat, olive-gray breast
and pale lemon-yellow belly. Bill dark
with pale base to lower mandible; tail
long, black and narrowly edged white.
Voice *Wit*.
Habitat Bushy mountain slopes.
Range Rocky Mountains, but not as far north as Alaska.
Movements Summer visitor.

Western Flycatcher
Empidonax difficilis
5–5½in/13–14cm

Identification Olive-brown above
with very bold eye-ring, but
relatively narrow wing-bars. Chin
and belly both yellow separated
by extensive olive breast. Tail is long
and lower mandible a clear orange.
Voice *Wee-seet* or *sweet*.
Habitat Woods and forests.
Range From Alaskan panhandle through western US.
Movements Summer visitor.

Eastern Wood Pewee

Contopus virens 6in/15–16cm

Identification Dull brown bird with crested crown; obscure, pale
eye-ring and narrow, pale, double wing-bar. Identical to Western
Wood Pewee, separated only by voice and distribution. Lower
mandible orange.

Voice *Pwee, pee-yer.*
Habitat Woods, margins, suburbs.
Range Eastern US and adjacent Canada.
Movements Summer visitor.

Western Wood Pewee

Contopus sordidulus 6in/15–16cm

Identification Virtually
indistinguishable from Eastern Wood
Pewee. Lower mandible may be all
dark, but also may be orange.
Voice *Peer;* also three note
swee-tee-tee.
Habitat Deciduous woods.
Range Western North America from Alaska to westernmost
Texas.
Movements Summer visitor.

Olive-sided Flycatcher

Contopus borealis

7–7½in/18–19cm

Identification Closely related to the wood pewees. A chunky flycatcher with stout bill and short tail. Upperparts brown with white tufts sometimes visible on inner part of wing. Heavily streaked breast and white throat are best field marks.

Voice A whistled *whip-three beers*.

Habitat Conifer bogs.

Range Boreal zone from Alaska to Newfoundland southwards through the Rockies and Great Lakes.

Movements Summer visitor.

Horned Lark

Eremophila alpestris   7–7½in/17–18cm

Identification Brown and buff streaked above, with black crown patch and horns, black through eye and black breast crescent. Face usually yellow, flanks usually streaked chestnut. The 'face' pattern is distinctive. Horns often difficult to see.

Voice A high-pitched *seee*.

Habitat Breeds among tundra, bare plains, mountains; winters on bare fields and along shorelines.

Range Breeds over most of Alaska and Canada south throughout most of US.

Movements Canadian birds move mainly into US; winter visitor only in south-east.

Barn Swallow
Hirundo rustica 6–6½in/16–17cm

Identification Metallic blue-black
above, rusty below. Long angled wings and deeply
forked tail with extended streamers in adult. Chestnut-
red face. Nests in rural buildings.
Voice High-pitched chatter.
Habitat Open farmland with buildings.
Range Temperate North America north to tree line.
Movements Summer visitor.

Cliff Swallow
Hirundo pyrrhonota 5–5½in/13–14cm

Identification Similar to Barn Swallow, but browner above with
distinct rusty rump; pale grayish below, with reddish face and dark
blue-black cap and throat; square tail. Easily separated from all
North American swallows except Cave Swallow which is rare in
south-west Texas. That bird lacks black throat of Cliff Swallow.
Voice Sweet single call.
Habitat Farms and/or cliffs.
Range Breeds virtually throughout North America except extreme
north and south-east, where, however, it is spreading.
Movements Summer visitor.

Violet-green Swallow
Tachycineta thalassina 4½–5in/12–13cm

Identification A 'black and white' swallow that shows an
iridescent green on back and inner wing only on a close approach.
Similar to Tree Swallow, but with white cheek extending above eye
so that it stands out; and white rump divided by black center. Tail
is square cut; flight more erratic than Tree Swallow.
Voice A twittering.
Habitat Woods, gardens.
Range Rocky Mountains to western coasts.
Movements Summer visitor, resident central California.

Tree Swallow
Tachycineta bicolor
5½–6in/14–15cm

Identification Dark metallic blue above, white below. Dark
upperparts extend below eye; no white on rump. Flaps and glides
in flight. Gregarious and widespread.
Voice Twittering.
Habitat Woodlands near water.
Range Breeds over most of Canada and northern US.
Movements Summer visitor; winters along eastern, southern and
western coasts; resident California.

Bank Swallow
Riparia riparia 4½–5in/12–13cm

Identification Small, brown swallow
with highly fluttering flight. Brown
above, whitish below with distinct
brown breast band. Tail distinctly
notched. Gregarious, forms dense
colonies. *See* Rough-winged
Swallow.
Voice A nasal, buzzed
twitter.
Habitat Sand cliffs.
Range Throughout North America
except extreme north and southern US.
Movements Summer visitor.

American Rough-winged Swallow
Stelgidopteryx serripennis 5–5½in/13–14cm

Identification A chunky,
longer-winged, less fluttering
version of the Bank Martin.
Chin, throat and breast are
dusky, lacking the well-defined
band of the more abundant bird.
Less gregarious than that species,
not colonial.
Voice A buzzing twitter.
Habitat Cliffs, river banks.
Range Throughout the US and southern Canada.
Movements Summer visitor, resident southern California and
Texas Gulf Coast.

Purple Martin

Progne subis 7½–8in/19–20cm

Identification Large, chunky
swallow with all-black
plumage in metallic
purple. Tail has
distinct 'V'. Female
has gray mottled underparts. Glides on broader wings than other
swallows.
Voice Deep twittering.
Habitat Common where multiple nest boxes are available.
Range Widespread in eastern US extending northwards through
Canadian prairies. Patchily distributed through Rockies, but
widespread along Pacific Coast.
Movements Summer visitor.

Blue Jay

Cyanocitta cristata 10–11in/26–28cm

Identification Common and widespread garden bird that is
obvious and relatively tame. Upperparts blue with distinct crest and
white bars across the wing. Long, black-barred tail, tipped white;
underparts gray with prominent dark chin-strap.
Voice Loud *jay-jay*.
Habitat Parks, gardens, forests.
Range Eastern US and eastern, southern Canada.
Movements Canadian birds move southwards.

Scrub Jay F
Aphelocoma coerulescens 10½–11½in/27–29cm

Identification Blue head, wings and tail are standard features, along with gray underparts. Color of back varies from pale to dark gray; that of chin from gray to white. Large bill and long tail are characteristic, as is a variably prominent breast band.
Voice Rasping *shreep*.
Habitat Suburbs, scrub, woods.
Range Rocky Mountain system of western US, plus Florida.
Movements Resident.

Pinyon Jay
Gymnorhinus cyanocephalus 10–10½in/25–27cm

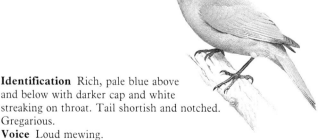

Identification Rich, pale blue above and below with darker cap and white streaking on throat. Tail shortish and notched. Gregarious.
Voice Loud mewing.
Habitat Pinyon-juniper forests of western mountains.
Range Central Rockies of US.
Movements Resident.

Gray Jay
Perisoreus canadensis 11–12in/28–30cm

Identification Dove gray above,
paler gray below. White on head,
'face' and neck variable, but always
the distinctive feature. Bill is short and
stubby, tail long. Common and
gregarious.
Voice *Whee-oo.*
Habitat Boreal Alaska and Canada,
southwards through north-eastern
US and the Rockies.
Movements Resident.

Black-billed Magpie
Pica pica 18–19in/46–48cm

Identification Large black and white bird with long, wedge-
shaped tail and green-blue gloss on wings and tail. Large black bill
on strong head; black above broken by white ovals on folded wings;
white below.
Voice Laughing and chuckling calls.
Habitat Woodland and brush country.
Range From southern Alaska southwards through prairies and
Rockies.
Movements Resident.

Clark's Nutcracker

Nucifraga columbiana 11½–12in/29–31cm

Identification Large, jay-like bird of mountain forests. Dove-gray above and below; black wings with white tipped secondaries and black and white tail. Pointed black bill; flies with crow-like flaps.

Voice Harsh *kra-a-a*.
Habitat Conifer forests in mountains.
Range US Rockies northwards into adjacent Canada.
Movements Resident, with periodic irruptions into semi-desert areas.

Common Raven

Corvus corax 23–24in/58–61cm

Identification Huge crow with heavy head, long and powerful bill and long, wedge-shaped tail that is particularly obvious in flight. Shaggy throat-feathers can be obvious both in flight and when perched.
Voice Deep croaking call.
Habitat Mountains, forests, tundra.
Range Throughout Alaska and Canada, save the prairies, and in western US and along Appalachians.
Movements Resident.

Chihuahuan Raven
Corvus cryptoleucus 19–19½in/48–50cm

Identification Larger than American Crow, but easily confused; slightly wedge-shaped tail, but smaller bill and head than Common Raven. Most easily distinguished by calls. Formerly called White-necked Raven, but the white bases of the neck feathers are usually obscured in the field.
Voice Low croak, higher pitched than Common Raven.
Habitat Arid lands.
Range South-western US.
Movements More northerly birds move southwards in winter.

American Crow
Corvus brachyrhynchos
16–17½in/41–45cm

Identification Large, all-black bird with powerful bill and square-shaped tail in flight. The North-western Crow is sometimes treated as a separate species. *See also* Fish Crow.
Voice Familiar *caw-caw*.
Habitat Very catholic, favoring wide range of habitats.
Range Most of sub-tundra North America. North-western Crow is found in coastal Alaska and British Columbia.
Movements Most Canadian birds move southward in winter.

Fish Crow
Corvus ossifragus 14½–15in/37–39cm

Identification Very similar to American Crow, but smaller with thinner bill.

Voice Nasal *cah* or *cah-cah*.
Habitat Shorelines, rivers.
Range Mainly near coast from New England to Texas.
Movements Inland populations tend to move to coast in winter.

Black-capped Chickadee
Parus atricapillus 4½–5in/12–13cm

Identification Buff-brown chickadee with black cap and white cheeks. Separate with care from Carolina Chickadee by white margins to flight feathers forming a distinct, pale wing-panel, and ragged lower edge to black bib. Hybridizes where ranges overlap.
Voice *Chick-a-dee-dee-dee.*

Habitat Gardens, woods, forest clearings.
Range Boreal Alaska and Canada extending southwards over northern half of US.
Movements Resident.

Carolina Chickadee
Parus carolinensis 4½in/11–12cm

Identification Similar to
Black-capped Chickadee, but
lacks pale panel in wing and
has neat, square-cut, black bib.
Voice High-pitched,
fast *fee-bee, fee-bee*.
Habitat Deciduous woods,
clearings, suburbs.
Range South-eastern US.
Movements Resident.

Boreal Chickadee
Parus hudsonicus 5–5½in/13–14cm

Identification Chunky chickadee, marked by chocolate-brown
cap, back and flanks; sooty wings and tail; bib black. The overall
impression is of a rather scruffy bird.
Voice Nasal *seek-a-da-da*.
Habitat Conifers.
Range Boreal Alaska and Canada.
Movements Resident.

Tufted Titmouse

Parus bicolor 6–6½in/16–17cm

Identification Gray above, white below, with a wash of warm rufous along the flanks. The plain face makes the dark eye a prominent feature as are the gray crest and black forehead patch. Birds from southern Texas have black crests and were formerly treated as a separate species.

Voice Repeated *peeta, peeta, peeta*.
Habitat Suburbs, parks, bush country.
Range Eastern US.
Movements Resident.

Verdin

Auriparus flaviceps

4½in/11cm

Identification Tiny, titmouse-like bird with fine, pointed bill. Adult is gray above, whitish below marked by yellow head and throat and a wedge of maroon at the bend of the wing. Juvenile is browner above and lacks the distinguishing features of the adult. It is thus similar to a Bushtit, but has a shorter tail and browner upperparts.
Voice *Chip-chip-chip* repeated.
Habitat Dry scrubland
Range All states bordering Mexico.
Movements Resident.

North American Dipper

Cinclus mexicanus 7–8½in/18–22cm

Identification A chunky, all-gray bird that is seldom, if ever, found far from tumbling, rocky streams. Rotund body, thick neck, short, rounded wings and tiny, often 'cocked' tail are best field marks. White eye-ring and stout yellow legs confirm. Perches on rocks, swims and wades in water.

Voice Loud song and characteristic *zeet* call.

Habitat Fast streams with boulders, long stony glides, weirs, etc.

Range Resident in western Alaska, Canada and US, in Rocky Mountain chain.

Movements Some local movement, especially where streams ice-up in winter.

White-breasted Nuthatch

Sitta carolinensis 5–6in/13–15cm

Identification Boldly-pied bird that climbs up and down trees with equal ease. Crown and nape are black, the remaining upperparts gray with black in wings and white corners to the tail. Underparts white with black eye standing out in contrast.

Voice A repeated nasal whistle *wee-wee-wee,* also a single *hank.*

Habitat Conifer, oak, juniper and other woodlands.

Range Resident US except where forests or woods absent. Just penetrates southern Canada.

Movements Resident in native woodland.

Red-breasted Nuthatch

Sitta canadensis 4½in/11–12cm

Identification: Equivalent of
White-breasted Nuthatch in
conifer forests, though the
two do overlap. Smaller with
black cap broken by bold
white eyebrow and black stripe
running through eye. Gray back,
with black and white tail.
Underparts a warm rust. Stripe
through eye is best field mark.

Voice Nasal *hank-hank-hank*

Habitat Conifer forests in north and in mountains of east and
west.

Range Breeds from north-western Canada to California, through
the Rockies and in narrow band across the border and Great Lakes
region. Also southwards from Newfoundland to the Appalachians.

Movements Irregular movements southwards across US when
food crops crash.

Brown-headed Nuthatch

Sitta pusilla 4½in/11cm

Identification Typical, short-tailed nuthatch, with blue-gray
upperparts and creamy-buff below. Distinguished by chocolate-
colored cap and black eye-stripe bordering white cheeks. Eastern
counterpart of Pygmy Nuthatch.

Voice Double squeak.
Habitat Loblolly pines.
Range South-eastern US from Texas to Virginia.
Movements Resident.

Brown Creeper
Certhia familiaris 5–6in/13–15cm

Identification Easily overlooked, brown and buff streaked bird, that climbs trunks and major limbs of trees. White underparts, long decurved bill and sharp-pointed tail-feathers are all good marks.
Voice High-pitched *see-see-see*. Attention is usually attracted by call than by a sighting.
Habitat All kinds of woodland and forest.
Range Breeds right across North America in conifer zone and southwards through Rockies and Appalachians.
Movements Winters throughout most of US as far as Gulf Coast.

House Wren
Troglodytes aedon
4½-5in/11-13cm

Identification: A widespread and common small wren. Chunky shape and short 'cocked' tail are characteristic. Upperparts only faintly barred and underparts paler than similar wrens. Generally grayer with no prominent facial marking.
Voice: A loud rising trill, plus various scolding notes.
Habitat: Broad-leaved woods, thickets,often alongside water.
Range: Breeds across US extending northwards into southern Canada.
Movements: Whole population moves southwards to winter along Gulf Coast, southwards to Mexico.

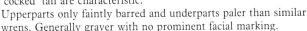

Winter Wren
Troglodytes troglodytes 4in/10cm

Identification Tiny, brown
bird very similar to House Wren.
Upperparts barred brown, buff
and black; underparts brown,
heavily barred on belly. Very short
tail often held cocked over back. House
Wren has longer tail and lacks barring on belly.
Voice Rich explosive warble.
Habitat Conifer woods with dense scrub.
Range Boreal Canada extending northwards into Alaska and
southwards along Pacific Coast and the Appalachians.
Movements Canadian birds migrate southwards to winter in
southern and eastern states.

Bewick's Wren
Thryomanes bewickii 4½–5in/12–13cm

Identification Well-marked wren with long, graduated tail, that is
wagged from side to side high above the back. Upperparts brown or
gray-brown with black barring on wings and tail; underparts white.
Bold white eyebrow and dark barring on ear coverts. Bill, long and
decurved.
Voice Buzzing warble.
Habitat Thickets, scrub, woodland clearings.
Range Breeds across southern US, but declining in the east.
Movements Largely resident, but eastern birds move southwards
to winter along Gulf Coast.

Carolina Wren
Thryothorus ludovicianus 5–5½in/13–14cm

Identification Medium-sized wren with plain, deep orange-cinnamon breast. Brown back, barred wings and tail; bold white eyebrow; mottled ear coverts.
Voice Pleasantly warbled three-note song.
Habitat Thickets in suburbs, stream sides, damp woods.
Range Southern and eastern US.
Movements Resident.

Rock Wren
Salpinctes obsoletus 5½–6in/14–15cm

Identification Crown, back and wings are gray, spotted white; rump and tail brown, and similarly spotted. Underparts whitish becoming creamy on belly; slight streaking. Short, pale eyebrow.
Voice *Tic-ear* and trilling.
Habitat Rocky gullies, hillsides.
Range Whole of western US and adjacent Canada.
Movements: Northern interior populations are migratory.

Canyon Wren
Catherpes mexicanus 5½–6in/14–15cm

Identification Easily identified by rufous body contrasting with gray crown and white face, throat and breast. But often difficult to see.
Voice Loud rich warble that stutters to a conclusion.
Habitat Dark canyons and gullies.
Range Rocky Mountains and foothills from Canadian border to central Texas.
Movements Some high-level breeders descend in winter.

Marsh Wren
Cistothorus palustris 5in/13cm

Identification Rich, rusty wren found in association with wetlands. Upperparts, rufous heavily barred black with series of bold white stripes on back. Crown, black-brown with lengthy, white eyebrow. Throat and upper breast, white. Formerly known as Long-billed Marsh Wren.
Voice Low *suk*.
Habitat Reed swamps.
Range Right across North America on both sides of Canadian border, locally in southern half of US.
Movements Mostly a summer visitor; winters in southern and coastal states.

Sedge Wren
Cistothorus platensis
4½in/11cm

Identification Similar to Marsh Wren, but has white streaked crown; faintly white streaked back, and buffy underparts. Pale eyebrow neither as bold nor as long as Marsh Wren. Formerly called Short-billed Marsh Wren.
Voice Chattering trill.
Habitat Shallow, overgrown marshes.
Range Breeds north-eastern US and southern Canada extending northwards into the prairies.
Movements Winters along Atlantic and Gulf coasts.

Northern Mockingbird
Mimus polyglottos 9–10in/23–25cm

Identification Dove-gray crown, back and rump; contrasting black wings and tail, both showing bold areas of white in flight and display. Underparts, pale gray. Bill, slightly decurved. Readily associates with suburban man.
Voice Accomplished mimic of other birds and natural and unnatural sounds.
Habitat Suburbs, thickets, open woodland.
Range Breeds across southern half of US and northwards along east coast.
Movements Northern interior birds move southward in winter.

Gray Catbird F.

Dumetella carolinensis 8½in/21–22cm

Identification Uniformly
slate-gray bird with black cap
and black tail that is often
held cocked over back. Rich
maroon undertail coverts.
Voice Cat-like *me-ou*.
Habitat Dense cover in woods and suburbs.
Range Breeds across southern Canada and much of US, though
absent from south-western quarter of the country and the Gulf
Coast.
Movements: Migratory, winters Florida and Gulf Coast and
along Atlantic Coast.

Brown Thrasher

Toxostoma rufum
10½–11½in/27–29cm

Identification Rich,
rufous brown above with
bold cream and black,
double wing-bar. Tail long
and rounded; bill decurved;
eye yellow. Underparts
cream, heavily streaked
black. Common bird
of woods and
hedges.
Voice Phrases repeated two or three times.
Habitat Woodland edges, suburbs, hedgerows.
Range Breeds throughout eastern US as far west as the Rockies
and northward into adjacent Canada.
Movements Winters in southern and Atlantic states.

Sage Thrasher

Oreoscoptes montanus 8½in/21–22cm

Identification A gray-brown thrasher heavily streaked below. Pale eyes; white, double wing-bar and pale tip to tail are all good field marks.
Voice Extended warbling with no mimicry.
Habitat Sage brush country, semi-desert.
Range Rocky Mountains and foothills in US.
Movements Migratory southward to winter in Mexico and bordering US states.

Curve-billed Thrasher

Toxostoma curvirostre 10–11in/26–28cm

Identification Large, gray thrasher with long uniformly dark, decurved bill (*see also* Bendire's Thrasher). Gray upperparts with double, white wing-bar; underparts heavily mottled, or virtually uniformly gray – never delicately streaked like Bendire's.
Voice Pleasant, variable warbling.
Habitat Hillsides, bushlands.
Range South-western US.
Movements Resident.

American Robin
Turdus migratorius 9½–10in/24–25cm

Identification Well-known, common bird marked by brown upperparts and rich-red underparts. Other field marks include boldly broken, white eye-ring, streaked white bib and white tips to the outer tail feathers. Juvenile shows same basic pattern, but is heavily spotted above and below.

Voice Melodic, three-note warble, repeated.
Habitat Suburbs, parks, woodland.
Range Breeds throughout North America.
Movements Canadian and north central US birds are migratory.

Townsend's Solitaire
Myadestes townsendi
8½–9in/21–23cm

Identification: A slender gray bird marked by short bill and pale eye-ring. Orange in wing, and white outer feathers of long tail are particularly obvious in flight. Perches openly, sometimes catching insects in the air. Juvenile is brown, spotted and barred above and below.
Voice: Pleasant warble.
Habitat: Mountain conifer forests.
Range: Rocky Mountains from Alaska to Mexican border.
Movements: Alaskan and Canadian birds move southward to winter.

Wood Thrush

Hylocichla mustelina 7½–8in/19–20cm

Identification Largest of the 'brown and spotted' thrushes. Upperparts are rich chestnut on crown and upper back, remaining parts brown. Underparts white, boldly-spotted black. Bold white eye-ring is excellent clinching field mark.
Voice Melodic three- to five-note phrases.
Habitat Deciduous and damp forests, suburbs.
Range Eastern US.
Movements Summer visitor.

Hermit Thrush

Catharus guttatus
6–6½in/16–17cm

Identification Small thrush with brown upperparts and rust-red tail. Underparts white with large splodges of brown and gray, particularly on the breast. Pale, narrow eye-ring. Colors vary somewhat across North America, but the rufous tail is virtually a constant feature. *See* other small thrushes and Veery.

Voice Fluty warble.
Habitat Woodlands, scrub.
Range Breeds through the boreal zone southwards through the Rockies.
Movements Most birds are migratory, though resident along the Pacific Coast throughout the year. Winters along the Atlantic and in southern US.

Swainson's Thrush
Catharus ustulatus 6½–7in/17–18cm

Identification Earth-brown above with
bold eye-ring and pale lores; underparts are
warm buff on breast, heavily-spotted with brown;
belly whitish, flanks brown-gray. Western form is a warmer
shade of brown.
Voice Rising series of whistles.
Habitat Wet scrub, thickets, damp woods.
Range Boreal and Rocky Mountain zones.
Movements Summer visitor.

Gray-cheeked Thrush
Catharus minimus 6½–7in/17–18cm

Identification Small, earth-brown thrush; white underparts
clearly spotted brown on the breast, and with a grayish wash along
the flanks. Uniform lores and ear coverts, together with
insignificant eye-ring, give this bird a somewhat featureless 'face'.
Voice Nasal, Veery-like song.
Habitat Conifer forests, also mixed woodland.
Range Northern taiga zone from Alaska to Newfoundland.
Movements Summer visitor.

Veery
Catharus fuscescens
6½–7in/17–18cm

Identification Warm rufous-
brown above, with warm buff on
throat and upper breast, delicately
streaked; white below with grayish
wash on flanks. Pale lores, and ear
coverts speckled. Rufous upperparts
separate from all other thrushes except
Pacific form of Swainson's Thrush.
Voice Series of fluty notes on a descending scale.
Habitat Damp woodlands and riverside thickets.
Range Breeds across the continent either side of the US-Canada
border, southwards through the Rockies and Appalachians.
Movements Summer visitor.

Eastern Bluebird
Sialia sialis 6½–7in/17–18cm

Identification Male is bright blue above; rusty below with white
belly and undertail. Female has only a touch of blue on the crown,
with bluish wings and tail; underparts a pale rust. Sits openly,
dropping to catch insects on the ground or in the air.
Voice Melodic *chur-lee*, repeated.
Habitat Woodland edges, clearings, orchards.
Range Eastern US and Canada.
Movements Birds from northern half of range migrate.

Mountain Bluebird
Sialia currucoides 6½–7in/17–18cm

Identification Male is blue above, with deep blue wings and tail; underparts pale blue becoming grayish on belly. Female is gray above and below, with blue in wings and tail. Plain featureless 'face' lacks eye-ring of other female bluebirds.
Voice A warbling *tu-lee*.
Habitat High level grasslands.
Range Western US as far north as Alaskan panhandle.
Movements Northern and interior birds migrate southward to Mexican border and beyond.

Blue-gray Gnatcatcher
Polioptila caerulea 4½in/11cm

Identification Small, long-tailed, active and conspicuous bird. Male is bluish-gray above with white eye-ring, black eyebrow, black wings, and long, black, white-edged tail. The underparts are pale gray.
Voice Nasal *wee*.
Habitat Woods, scrub.
Range Breeds across most of US, though absent from north-central and north-western states.
Movements Summer visitor, but resident along Atlantic and Gulf coasts and along Mexican border.

Black-tailed Gnatcatcher
Polioptila melanura 4½in/11cm

Identification Gray above with black cap, blackish wings and black tail with white margins. Female lacks black cap, but has much less white in tail than the Blue-gray Gnatcatcher.
Voice Repeated *gee*.
Habitat Arid brush country, sagebrush, etc.
Range US along Mexican border.
Movements Resident.

Golden-crowned Kinglet
Regulus satrapa 4in/10cm

Identification Tiny, ever-active bird, greenish above, with black wings marked by double, white wing-bar, and black tail. Male has complex 'face' pattern of black eyestripe, white eyebrow and vivid orange-red crest. Female is similar, but with yellow crest.
Voice Thin *see-see-see*.
Habitat Conifer woods.
Range Boreal Canada together with Rockies, Appalachians and northern US.
Movements Northern birds migrate to winter throughout US.

Ruby-crowned Kinglet

Regulus calendula 4½in/11cm

Identification: Similar to
Golden-crowned Kinglet with
greenish upperparts and black
wings with double, white wing-
bar. Both sexes show plain face,
lacking the distinctive stripes of
the Golden-crowned. Male has
red crest, but this is seldom a
prominent field mark.
Voice: Thin *see-see-see*.
Habitat: Conifer woods and thickets.
Range: Boreal Canada extending southwards through the US
Rockies.
Movements: Migratory, wintering southern, western and eastern
US.

Buff-bellied Pipit

Anthus rubescens
6−6½in/16−17cm

Identification Previously known as Water Pipit and as American
Pipit. A slim, long-tailed bird, brown-gray above, lightly streaked;
buffy below with fine streaking on the breast; much heavier
streaking in winter. White, outer tail feathers. Spends much time
walking; dark legs.
Voice Thin *pee-eet*.
Habitat Tundra, mountains.
Range Northernmost Canada extending southwards through
highest Rockies.
Movements Winters south to most areas of US, except the
interior.

Sprague's Pipit
Anthus spragueii 6–6½in/16–17cm

Identification Similar to Buff-bellied Pipit, but with pale margins to feathers of upperparts producing a 'scalloped' effect. Dark eye with no obvious stripes; streaking on breast clear-cut; belly white. More white on outer tail than Buff-bellied; pink not dark legs.
Voice Loud *squeet*.
Habitat Grasslands.
Range Canadian and US prairies.
Movements Summer visitor; winters Texas and adjacent states and into Mexico.

Bohemian Waxwing
Bombycilla garrulus 8–8½in/20–21cm

Identification Chubby, olive-brown bird with bold crest, dark 'face' pattern and black wings, with white bar. Tail is shortish and tipped yellow. Waxy marks on wings seldom obvious.
See Cedar Waxwing.
Voice Buzzy notes.
Habitat Conifer woods.
Range Alaska and western Canada.
Movements Regularly winters north-western US, but irrupts eastwards every few years to areas where it is otherwise unknown.

Cedar Waxwing
Bombycilla cedrorum 6½–7in/17–18cm

Identification Smaller, browner version of Bohemian Waxwing, with similar crest and cross 'face' pattern. Gray rump, white undertail and yellow belly are best means of distinction. Large flocks in winter.
Voice Quiet trilling.
Habitat Conifer and mixed woods.
Range Breeds right across temperate North America in a belt either side of the US-Canada border.
Movements Northern birds regularly migrate over whole of US.

Northern Shrike
Lanius excubitor 9–10in/23–25cm

Identification Medium-sized gray bird of predatory habits. Crown and back, pale gray with black wings and tail, white rump and black facial mask. Underparts lightly barred; bill large and hooked. Perches openly. In flight, shows bold white wing flash. *See* Loggerhead Shrike.
Voice Harsh *chack-chack*.
Habitat Open scrub north of boreal zone.
Range Sub-tundra zone of Canada.
Movements Resident south Alaska otherwise moves southward to winter across temperate Canada and US.

Loggerhead Shrike
Lanius ludovicianus
8½−9in/21−23cm

Identification Very similar to
slightly larger Northern Shrike.
Smaller bill; larger black mask
extends above eye and over base
of upper mandible; smaller, white
wing-patch; and darker shade of gray
are the main features to look for.
Voice Harsh *chack-chack*.
Habitat Brush covered areas of scrub.
Range Breeds throughout US northwards into temperate Canada.
Movements Canadian and birds of central northern states move
southwards to winter.

Starling
Sturnus vulgaris 8½in/21−22cm

Identification Introduced from Europe and now widespread.
Iridescent green and purple sheen on back in summer; heavily
spotted white and buff in winter. Short-tail, pointed wings and
yellow bill characteristic at all times. Gregarious and aggressive.
Voice Wheezes and mimicry.
Habitat Cities, villages, farmsteads, woods.
Range Temperate and boreal North America.
Movements Some movements, but found throughout breeding
range in winter.

Black-capped Vireo
Vireo atricapillus 4½in/11cm

Identification Black cap with bold-white eye-ring and white loral stripe of male precludes confusion with any other vireo. Female has slate-gray head and less boldly marked 'spectacles'. Small size; upperparts green; yellow wash on flanks; bold, double wing-bar. Tends to be secretive.

Voice Twittered and slurred notes.
Habitat Scrub.
Range Mainly central Texas.
Movements Summer visitor.

Solitary Vireo
Vireo solitarius 5–5½in/13–14cm

Identification: Widespread, but variable vireo. Eastern birds have gray heads, green upperparts and yellow-streaked flanks. Birds in the Rockies are gray; those on the West coast have olive-green heads. All have bold 'spectacles', double wing-bars and streaked (not washed) flanks.

Voice: Melodic *chu-eet, cheereo, chuwee*.
Habitat: Deciduous and mixed woods.
Range: From boreal zone southwards through the Rockies and through the Great Lakes and Appalachians.
Movements: Winters Florida and Gulf Coast.

White-eyed Vireo
Vireo griseus 4½–5in/12–13cm

Identification Olive gray above with double wing-bar, yellow-washed flanks and yellow spectacles. Eye is white, but difficult to see in the field.
Voice Slurred five- to seven-note warble beginning and ending *chip*.
Habitat Damp thickets.
Range Most of eastern US.
Movements Winters Florida and Gulf Coast.

Bell's Vireo
Vireo bellii 4½in/12cm

Identification: Olive-gray vireo, with white, double wing-bar and bold eye-ring. Variable plumage, some have indistinct eye-ring and only one faint wing-bar.
Voice Rapid warble of harsh notes.
Habitat Woodland and scrub.
Range South-western and central US.
Movements Summer visitor.

Yellow-throated Vireo
Vireo flavifrons 5–5½in/13–14cm

Identification Olive above, green on 'face' with yellow 'spectacles' and lores. Rump gray, breast yellow and belly white.
Voice Slow three or four-note song, repeated endlessly.
Habitat Edges, brambles.
Range Eastern US.
Movements Mostly summer visitor; some winter Florida and Gulf Coast.

Red-eyed Vireo
Vireo olivaceus
5½–6in/14–15cm

Identification Olive-brown upperparts marked by gray crown, black lateral coronal stripe, white supercilium and black eye stripe. Only Black-whiskered Vireo of coastal Florida can be confused. Red eye may be difficult to see in field. Yellow sub-species occurs in Texas.
Voice Variable song produced at great length.
Habitat Woods.
Range Eastern US extending northwards through the boreal zone of Canada.
Movements Summer visitor.

Philadelphia Vireo
Vireo philadelphicus
4½–5in/12–13cm

Identification Small version of Red-eyed Vireo, but lack of lateral crown stripe produces a less-prominent head pattern. Olive above, grayer on crown with bold-white supercilium and eye-stripe. Yellow breast is usually obvious.
Voice Slow, variable song.
Habitat Woodland clearings, riverside scrub.
Range Southern Canada from Alberta to St Lawrence.
Movements Summer visitor.

Warbling Vireo
Vireo gilvus 5–5½in/13–14cm

Identification Grayish vireo with washed-out, pale foreparts. Back is olive-gray, underparts white; bold supercilium and clear-gray eye-stripe. Lacks wing-bars like Red-eyed and Philadelphia Vireo.
Voice Pleasant warbling.
Habitat Deciduous woodland.
Range Most of vegetated North America, though absent from much of Texas.
Movements Summer visitor.

Black-and-white Warbler
Mniotilta varia 5–5½in/13–14cm

Identification Breeding male is
boldly black and white, marked
by black chin and ear coverts and
much streaking on breast and
flanks. Female lacks black chin
and has gray ear coverts. In all
plumages the striped crown is the
best field mark. Climbs tree trunks and branches like a nuthatch.
Voice Thin *wee-see*, repeated.
Habitat Woodlands.
Range Summer visitor to eastern North America extending
northwards through western Canada.
Movements Winters Florida and Gulf Coast.

Prothonotary Warbler
Protonotaria citrea 5½–6in/14–15cm

Identification Breeding male has plain yellow head, breast and
belly broken by large, dark eye. Wings and short, rounded tail are
gray. Female is less golden, particularly on head and nape.
Voice Loud *weet-weet*, repeated.
Habitat Stream-side woodlands, nests in cavity.
Range Eastern US, but seldom common.
Movements Summer visitor.

Swainson's Warbler
Limnothlypis swainsonii 5½–6in/14–15cm

Identification A dull brownish
warbler marked by long, dagger-like bill.
Olive-brown upperparts; buffy-cream
underparts. Best field mark is chocolate-
brown cap and dark eye-stripe separated
by broad, whitish supercilium. Hides in
cover.
Voice Series of slurred whistles rising at the end.
Habitat Dense thickets near water.
Range South-eastern US to northern Florida and eastern Texas.
Movements Summer visitor.

Worm-eating Warbler
Helmitheros vermivorus
5½in/13–14cm

Identification Olive-brown upperparts contrast with warm-
orange, buff head and breast. Black stripes through eye and along
sides of crown create a distinctive pattern similar to that of several
sparrows.
Voice Rapidly repeated *chip*.
Habitat Dense woodland thickets.
Range South-eastern US.
Movements Summer visitor, occasionally seen on migration
westwards to California.

Golden-winged Warbler

Vermivora chrysoptera 4½–5in/12–13cm

Identification Breeding male is gray above marked by yellow wing coverts and fore-crown. Black ear coverts and large bib create a unique face pattern. Female is similar, but with less extensive yellow in wing and on crown and with gray rather than black face pattern. Undertail shows white spots.

Voice A buzz of four of five notes.

Habitat Woodland margins and neglected grassland.

Range North-eastern US into southernmost Canada southwards through the Appalachians.

Movements Summer visitor.

Blue-winged Warbler

Vermivora pinus 4½–5in/12–13cm

Identification Male has yellow head and underparts broken by clear black stripe through the eye. The back is olive, the wings blue-gray with bold-white, double wing bar. The blue-gray tail has white spots visible from below. Often hybridizes with Golden-winged Warbler to create a wide range of intermediate types some of which are of regular enough occurrence to have been given names: e.g. Brewster's and Lawrence's Warblers.

Voice A buzzing similar to Golden-winged Warbler.

Habitat Scrub and regenerating woodland.

Range North-eastern US, but expanding.

Movements Summer visitor.

Bachman's Warbler
Vermivora bachmanii 4½–5in/12–13cm

Identification A neat olive-green and
yellow warbler marked by a gray crown
and broad, black breast band. Male has
black band across crown over the eye,
lacking in female: thin, decurved bill. Very rare indeed.
Voice Rapid buzzing.
Habitat Swampy woodland.
Range Close to extinction, may be confined to I'On Swamp,
South Carolina.
Movements Summer visitor; winters Cuba.

Tennessee Warbler
Vermivora peregrina 4½–5in/12–13cm

Identification Summer male has
olive-green upperparts, white underparts
and gray crown. Female lacks gray crown
and has yellow wash on breast. Non-breeding
birds are greener above and below with clear
supercilium, single wing-bar and white undertail
coverts.
Voice Repeated *seet* on descending scale.
Habitat Deciduous and mixed woodland, feeds in canopy.
Range Boreal zone of Canada and Alaskan panhandle extending
across US border in east.
Movements Summer visitor; winters Mexico to northern South
America.

Orange-crowned Warbler
Vermivora celata 5–5½in/13–14cm

Identification Dull, greeny-yellow warbler marked by lightly streaked underparts. The orange patch on the crown is seldom visible. Color varies from bright yellowish western birds, to dull olive eastern ones. Immatures are generally greener, like young Tennessee Warblers, but lack white undertail coverts of that bird.
Voice A repeated trill.
Habitat Thickets, open woodland, forest margins.
Range From Alaska through the boreal zone to Labrador and southwards throughout the Rockies.
Movements Winters mainly in Florida and along the Gulf Coast, but also along Atlantic and Pacific coasts.

Nashville Warbler
Vermivora ruficapilla 4½–5in/12–13cm

Identification Dark upperparts and yellow underparts. Female has darker, brownish head and lacks yellow on throat. Fall birds are duller still, with eye ring the only prominent feature.
Voice *See-weet*, high-pitched and repeated, followed by a trill.
Habitat Regenerating woods and damp spruce woodland.
Range Breeds north and south of the Canada-US border in eastern and western populations separated by a gap through the prairies.
Movements Summer visitor; winters southern, coastal California and south-west coast of Texas.

Yellow Warbler
Dendroica petechia 5–5½in/13–14cm

Identification Male
is yellow above and below,
liberally streaked chestnut on the
breast. Female is paler and greener,
without streaking. Fall birds are
similar to female and best identified by
pale spots in the spread tail.
Voice Six or seven *sweet* notes.
Habitat Damp thickets of willow as well as gardens.
Range Virtually throughout North America south of the tundra,
but absent much of Texas and Gulf Coast.
Movements Summer visitor; winters southern California.

Magnolia Warbler
Dendroica magnolia 5–5½in/13–14cm

Identification Breeding male is black above
with gray crown, white supercilium and black
mask. A bold, white, double wing-bar
merges to form a broad patch in the
closed wing. The underparts are
yellow, streaked black, the
streaks merging to form a
black band across the breast.
The rump is yellow and there are white patches
at the sides of the tail. The female has no black
mask or breast band, but is otherwise similar.
Fall birds have a gray crown, grayish breast band, pale supercilium,
double wing-bar and yellow rump.
Voice Musical warble.
Habitat Conifer woods.
Range Boreal North America, southwards through Appalachians.
Movements Summer visitor.

Cape May Warbler
Dendroica tigrina 5–5½in/13–14cm

Identification A dark, heavily-streaked warbler. Summer male is olive, streaked black, above; yellow, streaked black, below. Best field marks are white wing patch and yellow 'face' with chestnut ear coverts. Female is similar, but has narrow, double wing-bar and only an orange wash on the 'face'. Fall birds are paler versions, though male retains white wing patch. Yellow rump in all plumages.
Voice High pitched *see-see-see*.
Habitat Spruce forests.
Range Boreal Canada.
Movements Summer visitor.

Yellow-rumped Warbler
Dendroica coronata
5½–6in/14–15cm

Identification Formerly divided into Myrtle and Audubon's Warblers. Basically gray above, streaked black; white below with black breast band and flank streaks. Males have yellow on crown, sides of breast and (in some populations) on throat. Double, white wing-bar, often nearly forming a white wing panel. Female and fall birds are brownish with pale supercilium and streaked breast. Yellow rump in all plumages.
Voice Pleasant warbling.
Habitat Woodland.
Range Widespread in northern and western North America.
Movements Winters over much of southern, eastern and western US.

Black-throated Green Warbler
Dendroica virens
5–5½in/13–14cm

Identification Dark olive above and with black wings marked by double, white wing-bar. Underparts white with black breast band and flank streaks. Male has black throat joining breast band; female has yellowish throat.
Voice Wheezing *zee-zee-zee*.
Habitat Conifer and mixed woods.
Range Boreal Canada, north-eastern US extending southwards through Appalachians.
Movements Summer visitor.

Black-throated Blue Warbler
Dendroica caerulescens 5–5½in/13–14cm

Identification Male is dark blue above with black 'face', throat and flanks, and a white patch at the base of the primaries. The underparts are white. Female is olive above and orange-buff below, with pale supercilium and tiny pale patch at base of primaries.

Voice Slow wheezy notes.
Habitat Deciduous forests.
Range South-eastern Canada and north-eastern US extending southwards through Appalachians.
Movements Summer visitor.

Cerulean Warbler

Dendroica cerulea 4½in/12cm

Identification Male is darkish blue above with bold, double white wing-bar. Underparts are white with black streaking on flanks merging to form black breast band. Female is green on crown and back with yellowish supercilium, yellowish throat and breast and gray streaking on flanks. Immature is olive above and washed with yellow below.

Voice Buzzing song.
Habitat Marshes and damp woodlands.
Range Eastern US.
Movements Summer visitor.

Yellow-throated Warbler

Dendroica dominica 5½–6in/14–15cm

Identification Upperparts gray with bold, double, white wing-bar; underparts white with bold streaking (spotting) on flanks. Male has yellow throat and upper breast and white supercilium (sometimes yellow on lores), separated by black. This distinctive 'face' pattern is shared only with Grace's Warbler, but the present species has a white patch behind the ear coverts.
Voice Descending whistled notes.
Habitat Mixed and deciduous woods.
Range South eastern US.
Movements Winters Florida and Gulf Coast.

Blackburnian Warbler
Dendroica fusca 5–5½in/13–14cm

Identification A black and
yellow warbler, marked in the
male by a bright orange throat
and bold, white wing patch.
Immature male and female are
blackish-brown above with double,
white wing-bar. Head and breast are
yellow, broken by complex pattern of
black marks; underparts are pale yellow
with streaked flanks. Pale tail margins
in males and some females.
Voice High notes followed by thin trill.
Habitat Conifer, mixed and deciduous forests.
Range Eastern Canada extending across US border and through
Appalachians.
Movements Summer visitor.

Chestnut-sided Warbler
Dendroica pensylvanica 5–5½in/13–14cm

Identification Heavily streaked black and
gray above with yellow crown and broad, black eye stripe and
moustachial streak. Underparts, white with rich chestnut along
flanks. Female similar, but with less yellow and patchy chestnut. In
fall, yellowish-green above, grayish-white below with yellowish,
double wing-bar.

Voice A whistled six-note song
with accent on the second to last note.
Habitat Regenerating deciduous
woodland.
Range Eastern North America
either side of the US-Canada border.
Movements Summer visitor.

Bay-breasted Warbler
Dendroica castanea 5½–6in/14–15cm

Identification Male in summer
has black 'face' separating rich
chestnut crown and throat. The
chestnut extends to the breast and
flanks and there is a pale, buffy patch
at the rear of the ear coverts. The
upperparts are blackish with white,
double wing-bar; the underparts a warm
buff. Female has only a hint of chestnut washed
over the breast. Fall male retains chestnut flanks; juveniles are
olive-greenish with black and white wings.
Voice Run-together double note.
Habitat Conifers.
Range Boreal Canada.
Movements Summer visitor.

Blackpoll Warbler
Dendroica striata 5½–6in/14–15cm

Identification Similar to Black-
and-white Warbler, but cap
completely black, lacking coronal
stripe. Male streaked gray and
black above with double, white
wing-bar, white cheeks and
white underparts heavily
streaked black. Female and
fall birds are yellowish on
head and breast, heavily streaked.
Voice High-pitched *see-see-see*.
Habitat Coniferous woods.
Range Boreal Canada and north-eastern US.
Movements Summer visitor.

Pine Warbler
Dendroica pinus 5½–6in/14–15cm

Identification Male in summer has olive-green upperparts with double, white wing-bar. Underparts yellow with streaking on sides of breast. Female is duller, with less yellow. Fall birds are browner above. A rather undistinguished warbler with a heavy bill.
Voice A pleasant trilling.
Habitat Pine woods.
Range Eastern US and adjacent Canada.
Movements Winters southern and eastern US.

Prairie Warbler
Dendroica discolor 4½–5in/12–13cm

Identification Olive-green above with faint streaking on back; yellow below with clear black streaking on flanks. Male has black facial markings enclosing an area of yellow below the eye. Female has grayish ear coverts and clear yellow supercilium.
Voice An ascending buzz.
Habitat Scrub, open woods.
Range Eastern US to southern Canada.
Movements Summer visitor; winters Florida.

Palm Warbler

Dendroica palmarum 5½–6in/14–15cm

Identification Dark warbler, with brown upperparts, pale wing coverts and chestnut-brown cap. Eastern birds have yellow underparts washed with chestnut and liberally streaked brown; western birds have yellow only on breast and are streaked gray on white on belly. Spends much time on ground.
Voice Trilling.
Habitat Damp margins of conifer forests.
Range Boreal Canada.
Movements Winters Atlantic and Gulf coasts of US.

Ovenbird

Seiurus aurocapillus 6in/15-16cm

Identification A ground-dwelling forest warbler. Olive-brown above, with reddish, coronal stripe, bordered black. White underparts with black streaking. Legs pink.
Voice Distinctive *teacher-teacher*.
Habitat Deciduous forests.
Range Across boreal Canada and eastern US.
Movements Summer visitor; some winter Florida.

Northern Waterthrush
Seiurus noveboracensis 6in/15–16cm

Identification Similar to
Louisana Waterthrush, but with smaller bill, lack of buff on flanks
and, in particular, shorter and tapering pale supercilium.
Voice Series of loud notes terminating in a slur.
Habitat Damp woods, thickets.
Range Boreal Canada southwards through the Great Lakes and
north-eastern US.
Movements Summer visitor; a few winter southern Florida.

Louisiana Waterthrush
Seiurus motacilla 6in/15-16cm

Identification Dark olive-brown above, with white supercilium
extending and broadening to nape. Underparts white, heavily
streaked black with warm, buffy wash along flanks. Pale pink legs;
ground dwelling. *See* Northern Waterthrush.
Voice Usually three, clear notes followed by trill.
Habitat Woodland streams.
Range Eastern US southwards from Canadian border.
Movements Summer visitor; some winter Florida.

Common Yellowthroat
Geothlypis trichas 5–5½in/13–14cm

Identification Olive above and yellow below, marked in the male by bold, black facial mask. Bright red legs. Female lacks mask. Geographical variation affects mostly the amount of yellow on underparts; western birds being brighter than eastern ones.
Voice Repeated *witchy*.
Habitat Overgrown grasslands, thickets.
Range Whole of sub-tundra North America.
Movements Summer visitor, winters southern and coastal states.

Yellow-breasted Chat
Icteria virens 7½–8in/19–20cm

Identification Large, heavy, thickset warbler. Brown above, yellow below. Short, chunky bill with white loral stripe extending to white eye-ring; short white moustachial streak. Generally self-effacing.
Voice Chattering.
Habitat Thickets and scrub.
Range Whole of US except Great Lakes and Florida.
Movements Summer visitor.

Kentucky Warbler
Oporornis formosus 5–5½in/13–14cm

Identification Upperparts olive, underparts yellow. Dark cap and black moustache enclose bright yellow eye-ring. Long pink legs; feeds mainly on ground.
Voice A repeated *churee*.
Habitat Damp woodland.
Range Eastern US.
Movements Summer visitor.

MacGillivray's Warbler
Oporornis tolmiei 5–5½in/13–14cm

Identification Upperparts olive-green without wing-bars. Head, gray with broken, white eye-ring; breast gray, with black speckling in male. Underparts entirely yellow; legs red; bill short. *See* Mourning and Connecticut Warblers.
Voice Buzzing trill.
Habitat Scrub and thickets.
Range Western US and Canada as far north as Alaskan panhandle.
Movements Summer visitor.

Mourning Warbler
Oporornis philadelphia 5–5½in/13–14cm

Identification Very
similar to MacGillivray's
and Connecticut Warblers,
but distinguished by lack
of white eye-ring. Note:
this feature needs a close
approach to check positively
and does not apply to immature
birds. Breeding male is olive-green
above, yellow below, with gray head and breast, the latter spotted
black. Female as female MacGillivrey's, but lacking eye-ring.
Immature birds have white eye-ring and yellowish throats.
Voice Slurred, five-note warble.
Habitat Damp thickets.
Range Boreal Canada and Great Lakes area.
Movements Summer visitor.

Connecticut Warbler
Oporornis agilis 6in/15–16cm

Identification Similar to MacGillivray's and Mourning Warblers,
with olive-green upperparts, gray head and breast, and yellow
underparts. Has a clear, complete, white eye-ring in all plumages.
Larger than similar species, spending more time on the ground
where it walks rather than hops.
Voice Loud, accelerating, clear notes.
Habitat Damp conifer and other woods with dense ground cover.
Range Boreal Canada and US Great Lakes region.
Movements Summer visitor.

Hooded Warbler
Wilsonia citrina 5–5½in/13–14cm

Identification A green and
yellow warbler, marked in the
male by a black hood
surrounding a yellow face.
Female has residual male
pattern with only a faint black breast band. Immatures show a
yellow supercilium and white in the tail.
Voice Pleasant warble with slurred flourish.
Habitat Thickets among damp woodland.
Range Eastern US as far as eastern Texas.
Movements Summer visitor.

Wilson's Warbler
Wilsonia pusilla 4½in/12cm

Identification Male is greenish above and yellow below with neat
black crown patch; this feature is lacking in the female which can
easily be confused with other yellow warblers that lack wing-bars.
Female and immatures both similar to larger Hooded Warbler, but
lack white in the tail.
Voice Long series of *chip* notes on a descending scale.
Habitat Ground cover in dense, damp woodland.
Range Boreal Canada and southwards through the Rockies.
Movements Summer visitor.

Canada Warbler
Wilsonia canadensis 5–5½in/13–14cm

Identification Blue-gray
upperparts without wing-bars.
Underparts yellow marked by
clear black streaking on the
breast in the male. Bold eye-ring joined to base of bill. Female has
subdued brownish breast streaking and only a hint of a loral line
between eye-ring and bill. Immature resembles female.
Voice Pleasant, variable warbling.
Habitat Forests with dense secondary growth.
Range Boreal Canada extending southwards into north-eastern US
and along Appalachians.
Movements Summer visitor; winters South America.

American Redstart
Setophaga ruticilla 5–5½in/13–14cm

Identification
Male is black with white belly and
distinctive bands of orange-red at bend
of wing, across the flight feathers, and at
the base of the tail. Female is olive-green
with patches of yellow where the male is
red. Young male resembles female with yellow
rather than red patches, but is darker and with a hint of orange at
the bend of the wing.
Voice High notes ending in downslurred flourish.
Habitat Coverts and damp woods.
Range Most of North America except for north and south-western
states from Texas to Oregon.
Movements Summer visitor; a few winter southern Florida.

House Sparrow
Passer domesticus 6–6½in/16–17cm

Identification Also called English Sparrow. Male has gray crown, white cheeks and black bib. Upperparts streaked black and chestnut, underparts dirty, gray-cream. Female dully colored with distinct creamy supercilium.
Voice *Chirrup*, repeated.
Habitat Cities, towns, suburbs, farmsteads.
Range Whole of inhabited North America; introduced from Europe.
Movements Resident.

Bobolink
Dolichonyx oryzivorus 7–8in/18–20cm

Identification Summer male is boldly marked in black with a white bar across the wing, white rump, and a creamy hood on the nape. At other times it resembles the female and immature which are streaked black and buff above, and buffy below. The striped head pattern; stubby, sparrow-like bill; and pointed tail-feathers are the best field marks.
Voice Loud *bob-o-link*.
Habitat Grasslands.
Range Right across northern US and southern Canada.
Movements Summer visitor; migrates south-eastwards to South America.

Eastern Meadowlark
Sturnella magna 9½−10in/24−26cm

Identification Medium-sized bird of open grasslands. In summer, yellow underparts with black 'V'-shaped breast band are clear feature. At other times streaked upperparts, striped crown, pointed bill and yellow-washed underparts identify. *See* Western Meadowlark.
Voice Whistling *see-you-see-yer*.
Habitat Grasslands.
Range Eastern US and south-eastern Canada, extends as far west as southern Arizona.
Movements Northern birds migrate, others resident.

Western Meadowlark
Sturnella neglecta 9½−10in/24−26cm

Identification Very similar to Eastern Meadowlark and overlaps range. This bird is grayer and less contrasting and has more yellow on 'face'.
Voice Bubbling notes.
Habitat Grasslands, generally drier than Eastern.
Range From the Great Lakes westwards.
Movements Northern and eastern birds migrate to winter along Gulf Coast westwards.

Yellow-headed Blackbird

Xanthocephalus xanthocephalus 9½–10in/24–26cm

Identification Male is black with buffy-
yellow head and breast broken by black
around eye and lores. Small white patch in
wing and thick, pointed bill. Female similar,
but with orange-yellow breast and brownish head;
generally browner than male.
Voice Rasping buzz.
Habitat Marshes and farmland.
Range Westwards from Great Lakes through prairies and
southwards to Arizona.
Movements Summer visitor; winters Mexican border; resident
California.

Red-winged Blackbird

Agelaius phoeniceus 8½–9½in/22–24cm

Identification Male is all
black with red, bordered
yellow-buff, wing
patches. Young male
is scaled black with less pronounced
wing patches. Female is boldly
streaked black above and below
with a hint of reddish on the
wing. *See* Triclored Blackbird.
Forms huge flocks.
Voice *Kouk-la-ree.*
Habitat Marshes and fields.
Range Whole of sub-tundra North America.
Movements Canadian and northern US birds are summer visitors.

Rusty Blackbird
Euphagus carolinus 9–9½in/23–24cm

Identification Breeding male
is all black with long, pointed bill
and contrasting yellow eye. Female
is slate gray with mottling on breast.
Outside breeding season, all birds have
rusty tips to feathers of body, wing coverts
and tertials that gradually wear away to produce
the summer plumage.
Voice High pitched *coo-a-lee*.
Habitat Damp woods and marshes.
Range Boreal Alaska and Canada.
Movements Summer visitor; winters over whole of eastern US
except extreme north.

Brewer's Blackbird
Euphagus cyanocephalus 9–10in/23–25cm

Identification Male is black with
purple gloss on head and green
gloss on wings and body. The
eye is yellow. Female is dull
brown above and below, with
dark eye. Some fall males are rusty on the body,
but never so obviously as Rusty Blackbird.
Voice Harsh, wheezy song.
Habitat Parks, suburbs, farmsteads, woods.
Range Western US and Canada extending eastwards to Great
Lakes.
Movements Some northern populations move southwards in
winter.

Great-tailed Grackle

Quiscalus mexicanus

(M)18–19in/46–48cm,
(F)15–15½in/38–40cm

Indentification Male has
purple gloss over body, with
long, 'V'-shaped tail, the eye is
yellow. Female is brown above
buffy on throat and breast, with
shorter, wedge-shaped tail. *See*
Boat-tailed Grackle, formerly
regarded as conspecific.
Voice Squeaks and harsh calls.
Habitat Marshes and open scrubland.
Range South-western US from Texas to California.
Movements Some northern populations move southwards in
winter.

Boat-tailed Grackle

Quiscalus major

(M)16½–17in/42–4cm
(F)14½–15in/37–39cm

Identification Male is washed iridescent blue with long, 'V'-
shaped tail. Brown, not yellow, eye separate from Great-tailed
Grackle, though some have paler eyes than others. The smaller size
and rounded, not flat, crown are reliable features. Female is brown
above and warm brown below.
Voice Variety of squeals.
Habitat Salt marshes, sometimes freshwater margins.
Range Atlantic and Gulf Coasts.
Movements Resident.

Common Grackle

Quiscalus quiscula 12½–13½in/32–34cm

Identification Male is black
with longish, 'V'-shaped tail. At close
range a purple gloss on head and
wings may be visible, though
northern and western birds
show a blue gloss on the head
and a bronze gloss on breast
and back. Female is brown
with dark eye, but also has 'V'-shaped tail.
Voice Loud squeaks.
Habitat Suburbs, farms, fields.
Range Whole of North America, east of the Rockies.
Movements Northern and western birds are summer visitors.

Brown-headed Cowbird

Molothrus ater 7½–8in/19–20cm

Identification Distinguished from other
blackbirds by stubby bill and small size.
Male has chocolate head and black
body with greenish gloss. Female
is brown above and dirty buff
below, with dark streaking.
Forms large flocks.
Voice Harsh sqeaking.
Habitat Parks, suburbs, farms, woods.
Range Whole of sub-tundra North America.
Movements Northern and western birds largely summer visitors.

Orchard Oriole

Icterus spurius 7–7½in/18–19cm

Identification Small oriole. Male has black head, back and breast, chestnut body and black wings and tail. Female is greenish above with double, white wing-bar and greenish-yellow below. Female Northern Oriole has warm orange breast.
Voice Whistling and fluting calls.
Habitat Orchards, suburbs, woods.
Range Eastern US.
Movements Summer visitor.

Northern Oriole

Icterus galbula 8½–9in/22–23cm

Identification Formerly divided into Baltimore and Bullock's Orioles. Eastern male has black head, back and breast; black wings with a white bar; and black tail with rufous terminal margins. Body and rump are rich rufous. Western male (Bullock's) has rufous extending over 'face' and a bold, white wing patch. Female is brownish above and warm orange below, though western female is much paler, with warm wash only on breast.
Voice Fluty whistles.
Habitat Woods and suburbs.
Range Most of US and southern Canada.
Movements Summer visitor.

Scarlet Tanager

Piranga olivacea 7–7½in/18–19cm

Identification Male is brilliant
scarlet with black wings and tail
and whitish bill. Female is
greenish-olive above, yellowish
below with no wing bars. In winter, male is greenish yellow with
black wings and tail.
Voice Harsh whistling.
Habitat Deciduous forests.
Range Eastern US extending into southern Canada.
Movements Summer visitor.

Summer Tanager

Piranga rubra 8–8½in/20–21cm

Identification Male is bright
red with broad red margins to black
wing feathers. Needs to be separated with care from Hepatic
Tanager. Female is greenish-olive above with yellow underparts,
variably washed with warm orange.
Voice Warbling whistles.
Habitat Oak-pine woods and cottonwoods.
Range Right across southern US.
Movements Summer visitor.

Northern Cardinal
Cardinalis cardinalis 8½–9in/22–23cm

Identification Male is red with black 'face' and bib, conical pink bill, and sharply pointed red crest. Female is buffy-brown on head, underparts and back with red wings, tail and crest.
Voice Repeated whistled phrases.
Habitat Suburbs, woodland margins, marshy thickets.
Range Eastern US extending westwards along Mexican border.
Movements Resident.

Rose-breasted Grosbeak
Pheucticus ludovicianus 8–8½in/20–21cm

Identification Chunky, thick-set finch with massive white bill. Male is black above, white below with bright red breast. A white rump shows in flight. Female is brown above; buff streaked brown below.
Voice Whistled phrases.
Habitat Regenerating woods, waterside thickets.
Range North-eastern US extending into Canada and westwards through boreal zone.
Movements Summer visitor.

Black-headed Grosbeak

Pheucticus melanocephalus 8½in/21–22cm

Identification Male has black head,
black back and tail, and
black wings with double, white
wing-bar and primary patch. The rich
cinnamon underparts are diagnostic.
Heavy, conical bill. Female similar to
female Rose-breasted Grosbeak, but with
much lighter, more diffuse, streaking on breast.
Voice Whistled phrases.
Habitat Woodland margins and clearings.
Range Western US into adjacent Canada.
Movements Summer visitor.

Evening Grosbeak

Hesperiphona vespertina 7½–8½in/19–21cm

Identification Thick-set finch with massive, pale conical bill.
Male is a yellow bird, though the tail is black, and the wings boldly
marked black and white. Forehead and supercilium, lower back and
belly all yellow. Female is grayer.
Voice A House Sparrow-like chirp.
Habitat Breeds in conifer forests; visits feeding stations for
sunflower seeds in winter.
Range Breeds across southern Canada, extreme north-eastern US,
and southwards through Rockies.
Movements Southwards throughout northern half of US.

Blue Grosbeak
Guiraca caerulea 6–7½in/15–19cm

Identification Chunky, large-billed finch that is dark blue with rusty wing patches in male. Only other 'blue' finch is smaller, paler and lacks rust. Female resembles female House Sparrow, but is warm brown rather than gray and has two rusty wingbars.
Voice Song is rich warble; calls *klink*.
Habitat Hedgerows, thickets, damp grasslands and sorghum fields; roadside wires.
Range Summer visitor northwards across southern half of US, though absent from most of Rockies.
Movements Winters southwards to Central America.

Indigo Bunting
Passerina cyanea 5½in/14cm

Identification Male is only all-blue finch. Considerably smaller and more dainty than Blue Grosbeak, with tiny conical bill and paler, more turquoise, plumage, looks black in poor light. Female, rusty-brown with double wing-bar.
Voice Warbled song with repeated phrases.
Habitat Scrub, wasteland, bushy pastures, neglected farmland.
Range Summer visitor to eastern US.
Movements Winters from Mexico to Panama.

Lazuli Bunting

Passerina amoena 5–5½in/13–14cm

Identification Similar in shape
and behavior to Indigo Bunting,
which it replaces in the west. Male
is blue on head, neck and rump;
breast and flanks warm rufous; belly
white. Bold, white, double wing-bar.
Female, warm brown. White wing-bars
separate from female Indigo Bunting.
Voice Descending and rising warble with
repeated phrases confined to opening notes.
Habitat Arid gullies with brush, poor pastures.
Range Summer visitor western US, though absent from southern
arid Rockies.
Movements Winters Mexico.

Painted Bunting

Passerina ciris 5½in/14cm

Identification Male is
highly colorful with purple
head, yellow-green back,
red rump and underparts. Bill
conical and silver; eye with red ring. Female
greenish above, yellowish-green below; pale eye-ring.
Voice Variable, mainly clear warbling.
Habitat Hedgerows, thickets.
Range Summer visitor to southern US as far north as Missouri.
Movements Winters Central American, though some stay on in
Gulf states.

Purple Finch
Carpodacus purpureus 6in/15–16cm

Identification Male is a rosy-pink on head, back and underparts, with pinkish margins to the wing feathers. Female is streaked brown on buff above and below creating a highly contrasting, striped impression. In particular, the pale supercilium is more prominent than in related species.
Voice Pleasant warble.
Habitat Conifer and mixed woodland.
Range Boreal Canada extending southwards through Rockies and the Great Lakes area to north-eastern US.
Movements Boreal zone birds move southwards to winter throughout eastern US.

House Finch
Carpodacus mexicanus 6in/15-16cm

Identification: Male has red band extending from forehead over eye, and a red breast. Crown and upperparts are brown; belly buff, streaked brown. Bill is short and stubby. Female is brownish streaked dark brown above and below.
Voice: Warbling with some nasal notes.
Habitat: Dry ranchland, suburbs and hillsides to considerable altitude.
Range: Western US; introduced in east where spreading rapidly southwards.
Movements: Resident, but may winter in new areas prior to colonization.

Pine Grosbeak
Pinicola enucleator
9–10in/23–25cm

Identification Largest of the 'red'
finches, with chunky shape
accentuated by smallish head
and bill. Male is red above
and below, with black tail,
and black wings marked by white,
double wing-bar. Female lacks red and
is warm orange-buff on head and nape,
otherwise gray.
Voice Low warbling with nasal ending.
Habitat Conifer woods, also deciduous woods in winter.
Range Boreal Canada to north-eastern US and southwards
through the Rockies.
Movements Northernmost birds move southwards on irregular
irruptive pattern.

Hoary Redpoll
Carduelis hornemanni 5½–6in/14–15cm

Identification High arctic
equivalent of Common Redpoll, which it closely
resembles. In general, a washed-out version with pale,
buff upperparts, white rump and whitish underparts. Pink wash on
breast of male, paler and less obvious.
Voice Buzzing trills.
Habitat Tundra.
Range Northern Alaska and Canada.
Movements Resident, but regularly seen southwards in Canada.

Common Redpoll
Carduelis flammea 5in/13cm

Identification Neat, arboreal finch with pink breast in summer male. Both sexes have red on crown and black bib, throughout the year. Upperparts streaked brown and buff; underparts buffy with brown streaking on flanks. Bill tiny and horn colored.
Voice Buzzing, nasal calls and trilled song.
Habitat Conifers, birches, taiga.
Range Alaska and northern Canada.
Movements Taiga birds move southwards to winter.

Pine Siskin
Carduelis pinus 5in/13cm

Identification Streaked brown and black above, brown and white below. Black wings show double wing-bar and yellow flash on primaries that is particularly prominent in flight. Thin, pointed bill.
Voice Wheezy, husky twittering.
Habitat Conifer and mixed woodland.
Range Breeds across boreal Canada and northern US to Alaskan panhandle and southwards through Rockies.

American Goldfinch
Carduelis tristis 5in/13cm

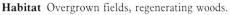

Identification Breeding male is bright
yellow with black crown, black tail,
and black wings marked by white,
double wing-bar. Female is green
above, pale yellow below with
white, double wing-bar. In
winter, the male is brown
above with yellow confined
to the 'face' and throat, the
female is similar, but grayer.
Voice Trilling warble.
Habitat Overgrown fields, regenerating woods.
Range Breeds through all but southern US, extending northwards
across the Canadian border.
Movements: Northern birds move southwards in winter, when
the species occurs in southern states.

Lesser Goldfinch
Carduelis psaltria 4½in/11cm

Identification Small
finch with stubby black
bill. Male has black cap
extending, in eastern birds,
over entire upperparts. In
western birds, the back is
green, contrasting with black
wings and tail. Underparts
are yellow. Wings show
white wing-bar, tips to tertials
and primary patch. Female is green above, yellow-buff to white
below with similar white marking on black wing.
Voice Trilling warble.
Habitat Fields, farms, hedgerows.
Range Western US.
Movements Birds in mountains move out in winter.

Red Crossbill
Loxia curvirostra 6–6½in/16–17cm

Identification Male
is red with brownish
wings and tail. Large
head and crossed
mandibles. Female
greenish-yellow. Size,
as well as size of bill, varies
considerably. In flight, short
tail and thick neck creates a
curiously chunky silhouette.
Voice Warbling; distinct *jip* in flight.
Habitat Coniferous forests.
Range Boreal Canada southwards through Rockies.
Movements Irruptive across much of US on irregular basis.

White-winged Crossbill
Loxia leucoptera 6½–7in/17–18cm

Identification Similar to Red
Crossbill, but marked in both sexes
by bold, white, double wing-bar.
Note white tips to tertials and
smaller head and bill.
Voice Warbles, *chet-chet* in flight.
Habitat Coniferous forests.
Range Boreal Alaska and Canada to northern Pacific US.
Movements Irregular, irruptive movements southwards over
much of northern half of US.

Dickcissel
Spiza americana 6–6½in/16–17cm

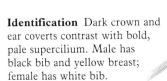

Identification Dark crown and
ear coverts contrast with bold,
pale supercilium. Male has
black bib and yellow breast;
female has white bib.
Upperparts streaked chestnut and black. In all adult plumages
there is a chestnut patch at the bend of the wing. Bill
black, thick and chunky.
Voice *Dick-dick-dickcissel.*
Habitat Fields and grasslands.
Range From the prairies eastwards to the Appalachians and
southwards to the Texas Gulf Coast.
Movements Summer visitor.

Rufous-sided Towhee
Pipilo erythrophthalmus 8½–9in/22–23cm

Identification Most widespread
towhee. Male is black
on head, breast and
upperparts with white panels
in the wing and white tips
to the long tail. Western
birds are flecked white on
wings and scapulars.
Underparts are white with rufous, chestnut flanks.
Female is brown above, white below with chestnut flanks; the
western female has similar white flecking as the male.
Voice *Tow-whee.*
Habitat Scrub and thickets, woodland edges and clearings.
Range Breeds over most of US and adjacent Canada, though
absent from most of Texas.
Movements Central birds are summer visitors; elsewhere resident;
winters Texas.

Brown Towhee
Pipilo fuscus 8½–9in/22–23cm

Identification Brown above and creamy below with large, conical, silver and black bill. Best field marks are a creamy bib enclosed by a necklace of black spots, and rufous, undertail coverts.
Voice Trills and hard, sharp *chinks*.
Habitat Dry brush areas, chaparral, suburbs, usually at some altitude.
Range South-western and Pacific coasts.
Movements Resident.

Savannah Sparrow
Passerculus sandwichensis 5½–6in/14–15cm

Identification A brown and buff streaked sparrow with shortish tail and some yellow on the 'face'. Highly variable coloration, but all birds have a prominent supercilium (often yellow); a bold, double moustachial streak; and pale coronal stripe. Otherwise they may be heavily streaked, as in California; plain backed and lightly streaked below, as in Colorado; or totally washed out, as in the formerly specific Ipswich Sparrow of Nova Scotia.
Voice A repeated *chip* followed by a trill.
Habitat Open ground.
Range From tundra to southern California, but absent from many southern states.
Movements Mainly summer visitor; winters southern and coastal states.

Grasshopper Sparrow
Ammodramus savannarum 5–5½in/13–14cm

Identification A short-tailed, large-headed sparrow of chunky appearance and proportionately large bill. Streaked above; plain buffy below with light flank-streaking only in some subspecies. Most have a clear coronal stripe.
Voice Double *chip* followed by a buzz.
Habitat Grassland.
Range Breeds over most of US and border Canada, though absent from large areas of the west.
Movements Summer visitor; winters Atlantic and Gulf Coast states and along Mexican border.

Baird's Sparrow
Ammodramus bairdii 5½–6in/14–15cm

Identification A well-marked, chunky sparrow with clear-cut pattern of head stripes. 'Face' is usually warm buff with coronal stripe, lateral stripe, broad supercilium, double moustachial streak, and white bib bordered below by neat rows of streaks that extend over the breast and continue along the flanks. This is a species that exhibits almost all the facial markings by which sparrows are identified. Upperparts are streaked buff and brown, with rich chestnut on the scapulars.
Voice Warble and trill.
Habitat Prairies.
Range Prairies either side of Canadian border; scarce and declining.
Movements Summer visitor; winters Arizona and adjacent Mexico.

Henslow's Sparrow
Ammodramus henslowii
5in/13cm

Identification
A thick-set, large-
headed sparrow with rich-chestnut
upperparts. Olive-gray head with
yellow-buff coronal stripe, double
moustachial streak, and neat, white bib. Nape
is plain olive-gray forming a half collar. Upperparts chestnut;
underparts buffy, with neat streaks on breast and flanks.
Voice *See-lic.*
Habitat Damp fields.
Range North-eastern US.
Movements Summer visitor; winters Florida and Gulf Coast.

Le Conte's Sparrow
Ammodramus leconteii
5in/13cm

Identification Easily identified
if well seen. Combination of white
coronal stripe, black lateral crown
stripe and broad, orange
supercilium separate from all other sparrows. White underparts
with orange breast band is shared only with Sharp-tailed Sparrow
which is always darker above. Generally very secretive.
Voice Buzzing.
Habitat Damp grassland.
Range Canadian prairies and grasslands.
Movements Summer visitor; winters Gulf Coast and adjacent
states.

Sharp-tailed Sparrow
Ammodramus caudacutus 5in/13cm

Identification Dark chestnut above, usually with fine white streaking. Whitish below with warm buff-to-orange wash on breast, sometimes streaked. Best field marks are gray coronal stripe and nape, and broad, orange supercilium. Considerable color variation.
Voice A trill.
Habitat Shorelines, lake margins.
Range Breeds across Canadian prairies and along Atlantic Coast of US.
Movements Prairie birds are summer visitors wintering along Florida and Gulf Coasts. Atlantic birds are resident.

Seaside Sparrow
Ammodramus maritimus
6in/15−16cm

Identification Highly variable and formerly divided into several distinct species: Seaside Sparrow, Cape Sable Sparrow, Dusky Seaside Sparrow. All have thinish, pointed bill; short, pointed tail; and yellow patch between bill and eye. Head, though variable in coloration, is plain rather than heavily marked like many other sparrows; all have a moustachial streak. Gulf Coast birds have yellow on head and chestnut backs; Atlantic birds are much grayer.
Voice Buzzing.
Habitat Tidal marshes.
Range Atlantic and Gulf coasts of US.
Movements Resident.

Vesper Sparrow
Pooecetes gramineus
6–6½in/16–17cm

Identification Well-streaked sparrow with short, white-edged tail. Lacks prominent supercilium of many other sparrows, but has dark ear coverts and clear moustachial streak. Chestnut shoulder patch usually difficult to see.
Voice Pleasant trilling.
Habitat Grasslands, farmsteads.
Range Breeds over most of temperate North America, though absent from southern states.
Movements Summer visitor; winters southern states.

Lark Bunting
Calamospiza melanocorys 7–7½in/18–19cm

Identification Male in summer is black, with thick, chunky bill and broad white wing patches. Female is brown above and streaked below, with broad buff wing patch and buffy supercilium extending around ear coverts. Winter male resembles female, but with white supercilium and moustachial streak joining to enclose dark ear coverts. Some black on throat and upper breast.

Voice Whistling trills, often in flight.
Habitat Dry grassland.
Range Central US and adjacent Canadian prairies.
Movements Summer visitor; winters Texas and Mexican border.

Lark Sparrow
Chondestes grammacus
6½–7in/17–18cm

Identification Brown above,
grayish below with distinctive
head pattern and small black
patch on breast. Crown and face
shows pattern of stripes in
chestnut black and white. In
flight, white outer feathers
contrast with black tail.
Voice Extended trills and buzzes.
Habitat Prairies and other open areas.
Range Most of US except eastern coastal states; also south-west
Canada.
Movements Summer visitor; winters Florida, Gulf Coast and
Mexican border states.

Black-throated Sparrow
Amphispiza bilineata 5½in/14cm

Identification Neat brown and white bird, marked by black bib
extending to a point on the breast. Brown head shows contrasting
white supercilium and moustachial streak. Immature has gray head
with bold white supercilium. White in outer tail, small bill.
Voice Trilling.
Habitat Dry hillsides.
Range Rocky Mountains from Oregon southwards.
Movements Northern birds move southwards in winter.

Dark-eyed Junco
Junco hyemalis
6–6½in/16–17cm

Identification Former division into four distinct species indicates variability of plumage. Male has gray upperparts extending to breast, with paler or white belly. Head may be black; back may be brown; belly may be washed pinkish. Most have pale, conical bill, and dark eye. Female is brown above and white below. All have broad white margins to tail.

Voice Pleasant trill.

Habitat Woodlands in summer; catholic in winter.

Range From Alaska to Newfoundland southwards, through northern US extending south through Rockies and Appalachians.

Movements Northern birds move southwards to winter throughout US.

Cassin's Sparrow
Aimophila cassinii
6in/15–16cm

Identification Chunky sparrow with heavy bill and long, white-tipped tail. Streaked crown and back; plain buffy underparts lack streaking, with white bib. Self-effacing.

Voice Whistles and trills.

Habitat Dry grasslands.

Range South-western states.

Movements Resident along Mexican border; more northerly birds move southwards to winter.

Bachman's Sparrow
Aimophila aestivalis 6in/15–16cm

Identification Large-billed, large-tailed sparrow. Crown and back gray, broadly streaked black; chestnut on wings. Underparts grayish with moustachial streak. Variable with western birds having much more chestnut, warm buff underparts, and largely lacking crown stripes.
Voice Warbled trill.
Habitat Pines and other dry woods.
Range South-eastern US.
Movements Northern interior birds move southwards for the winter.

American Tree Sparrow
Spizella arborea 6–6½in/16–17cm

Identification Attractive, delicately colored sparrow. Upperparts are streaked, rich chestnut with prominent white, double wing-bar. Underparts pale gray, extending to sides of head. Most obvious field marks are chestnut cap and chestnut smudge at side of breast. Thin line extends from behind eye; small black patch at center of breast.
Voice Thin warble.
Habitat Taiga with scattered trees; winters marshes and neglected fields.
Range Northern Canada and Alaska.
Movements Summer visitor; winters over most of US.

Chipping Sparrow
Spizella passerina 6in/15–16cm

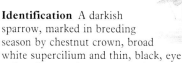

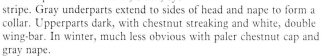

Identification A darkish
sparrow, marked in breeding
season by chestnut crown, broad
white supercilium and thin, black, eye
stripe. Gray underparts extend to sides of head and nape to form a
collar. Upperparts dark, with chestnut streaking and white, double
wing-bar. In winter, much less obvious with paler chestnut cap and
gray nape.
Voice Rapid, trilling, *chip-chip-chip*.
Habitat Suburbs, farmland.
Range Virtually the whole of vegetated North America.
Movements Largely a summer visitor, but resident in southern
states.

Clay-colored Sparrow
Spizella pallida 5½–6in/14–15cm

Identification Neatly marked
sparrow with unstreaked underparts.
Head shows buffy coronal stripe; dark
lateral streaking; broad, white
supercilium; darkish ear coverts;
and neat moustachial streak on
white bib. Underparts are warm
buffy.
Voice Buzzing.
Habitat Prairies, thickets.
Range Prairie Canada and adjacent
US eastwards through Great Lakes
region.

Movements Summer visitor; winters south-west Texas and
beyond.

Harris' Sparrow

Zonotrichia querula 7½–8½in/19–21cm

Identification Large, long-tailed, pink-billed sparrow. In summer, has black crown and bib contrasting with gray sides of head, marked with a black comma. In winter, sides of head are buffy. Upperparts neatly striped black and buff with bold, double wing-bar. Underparts white in summer, but with buffy flanks in winter.
Voice Extended whistles.
Habitat Taiga; in winter open scrub.
Range North-western Canadian arctic.
Movements Winters central US.

White-crowned Sparrow

Zonotrichia leucophrys 7–7½in/18–19cm

Identification Streaked buff and brown above; unstreaked grayish below extending to sides of head and nape. Distinctive crown pattern of black and white stripes; only White-throated Sparrow shows similar pattern in some area. Conical, pink bill.
Voice Whistles and trills.
Habitat Open areas, scrub, grassland.
Range Breeds across northern Canada and Alaska and southwards through the Rockies.
Movements Southern Rocky Mountain birds are resident; northern populations winter over much of US.

White-throated Sparrow
Zonotrichia albicollis

6½–7in/17–18cm

Identification Large, ground-
dwelling sparrow with typical
hunched appearance. Bold
pattern of head stripes similar to White-crowned Sparrow, but in
some birds coronal stripe is gray and eyebrow a warm buff. In
others, these may be white as in White-crowned, but with a yellow
area at the front of the supercilium. White bib and rich chestnut
upperparts are both useful features.
Voice Thin *dee-dee, diddla-diddla-diddla*.
Habitat Thickets in woodland and suburbs.
Range Breeds over much of temperate and boreal Canada into the
north-eastern US.
Movements Summer visitor; winters through much of lowland
US, especially in the east, but also in coastal California. Resident
north-eastern US.

Fox Sparrow
Passerella iliaca 7–7½in/18–19cm

Identification Variable both in
plumage and structure. Most have
rusty rump and tail, many have gray
crown and back, all have spotting
or streaking on underparts.
Voice Whistling and buzzing.
Habitat Undergrowth in woodland.
Range Boreal Canada and Alaska southwards through Rockies.
Movements Summer visitor; winters Pacific Coast and across
southern states.

Lincoln's Sparrow
Melospiza lincolnii 6in/15–16cm

Identification: Neatly streaked
brown and black upperparts,
with chestnut in the wing,
contrast with whitish belly.
Breast is warm buff, finely
streaked black. Head pattern
has gray coronal stripe, with
chestnut and black lateral
crown stripes and a broad, gray
supercilium; dark ear coverts and thin moustachial streak.
Somewhat secretive.
Voice Pleasant trilling.
Habitat Marshes and grasslands in summer; dense thickets in
winter.
Range Boreal Alaska and Canada extending southward into the
Great Lakes region and through the Rockies.
Movements Summer visitor; winters southern US; resident
Pacific US.

Swamp Sparrow
Melospiza georgiana
6in/15–16cm

Identification A well-marked, rather
dark sparrow. In summer has rich
chestnut cap that is absent in winter.
At all times the gray face, with double
moustachial streak, gray supercilium
and white bib are characteristic.
Shows more chestnut in wings and
on rump than other sparrows.
Underparts gray with chestnut streaked flanks.
Voice Pleasant trill.
Habitat Well vegetated marshes.
Range Temperate Canada and north-eastern US.
Movements Summer visitor; winters southern states; resident
north-east US.

Song Sparrow
Melospiza melodia 6–6½in/16–17cm

Identification Though highly
variable, all Song Sparrows have a
broad, gray supercilium; dark,
moustachial streak; long, rounded tail,
and spotting or streaking on the breast.
Most show chestnut in the wings and the
breast streaking, though variable, usually
forms a solid spot on the breast.
Voice Varied clear notes followed by a trill.
Habitat Scrub and waterside thickets.
Range Most of North America, except southern US.
Movements Northern birds are summer visitors; winters southern
US.

McCown's Longspur
Calcarius mccownii 6in/15cm

Identification Summer male has black cap, moustachial streak
and crescent-shaped breast band. Otherwise rather gray. Female is
buffy, with broad supercilium and hint of breast band. In winter,
both sexes are buffy, the male with a remnant breast band. Thick
bill, chestnut patch at bend of wing and black-tipped, white tail are
standard in all plumages.
Voice Warbles in song flight.
Habitat Prairies.
Range Prairies either side of US-Canada border.
Movements Summer visitor; winters northern and western Texas
and adjacent states.

Chestnut-collared Longspur
Calcarius ornatus 6in/15–16cm

Identification Unmistakable when
breeding. Crown, margins to ear coverts
and underparts all black; 'face' yellow;
nape chestnut. In winter, buffy with
black scaling on underparts; female
buffy. Grayish-white tail, tipped black.
Voice Melodic warbling.
Habitat Prairies.
Range Prairies both sides of US-Canada border.
Movements Summer visitor; winters north and eastern Texas to
southern New Mexico.

Lapland Longspur
Calcarius lapponicus 6–6½in/16–17cm

Identification Summer
male has black head and
breast broken by white line
behind the eye that extends
as margin to black throat and
breast. Chestnut nape. Female
duller, but with chestnut nape.
In winter, loses much of summer
plumage, or with chestnut nape in
others. Always shows much chestnut
in wings in winter.
Voice Warbling in flight.
Habitat High tundra; winters shores and stubbles.
Range Arctic Alaska and Canada.
Movements Winters across most of US, but not Rockies or
southern states.

Smith's Longspur

Calcarius pictus 6–6½in/16–17cm

Identification Summer male is rich
orange below, with orange nape and
richly streaked back. Head is black,
with broad white supercilium
and cheek patch producing
unique pattern. Female and
winter male have striped crown,
buffy supercilium and warm buff
underparts, lightly streaked black.
White outer tail feathers.
Voice Warbling ending in a flourish.
Habitat Tundra.
Range Extreme arctic Canada and southern Alaska.
Movements Summer visitor; winters in lower Mississippi area.

Snow Bunting

Plectrophenax nivalis 6½–7in/17–18cm

Identification In all plumages, shows white inner wing in flight.
Summer male is white with black back, wings and central tail. In
winter, both sexes have buff washed crowns, with warm buffy tones
on sides of head and breast.
Voice Pleasant warble.
Habitat Tundra.
Range Northern Alaska and Canada.
Movements Summer visitor; winters from southern Alaska and
Pacific Canada across whole of US and southern Canada.

Index